HIPPOCRENE DICTIONARY
AND PHRASEBOOK

BRITISH-AMERICAN

AMERICAN-BRITISH

Also by Catherine McCormick:

Language and Travel Guide to Britain

HIPPOCRENE DICTIONARY
AND PHRASEBOOK

BRITISH-AMERICAN

AMERICAN-BRITISH

Catherine McCormick

HIPPOCRENE BOOKS
New York

For information, address:
HIPPOCRENE BOOKS, INC.
171 Madison Avenue
New York, NY 10016

Cataloging-in-Publication Data

McCormick, Catherine M.
    British-American/American-British : Hippocrene dictionary and
phrasebook / Catherine McCormick.
        p.   cm.
    ISBN 0-7818-0450-7
    1. English language--Great Britain--Glossaries, vocabularies, etc.
2. Americans--Travel--Great Britain--Handbooks, manuals, etc.
I. Title.
PE1704.M38 1996   96-7636
423'.1--dc20   CIP

For Phil, Rae, Mary and Frances

Contents

Acknowledgments	9
Introduction	11
How to Use This Book	13
Travel Tips	15
Five-Minute History of the UK	19
Map Key	22
Map of the United Kingdom	23
Two Minute Tour of the UK	24

British-American Dictionary	27
American-British Dictionary	73
Phrasebook	117

Travel Essentials	117
Accommodation	117
Currency	118
Chunnel	119
Disabled, Facilities for	120
Driving	120
Electricity	122
Health	123
Post Office	124
Telephone	124
Time	126
Tipping	127
Trains	127
VAT (Value Added Tax)	128
Weather	128
London	129
London, as Home Base	129
London, Transportation	130
The People	130
Architecture and Archaeology	130
Crime and Police	132
Holidays	134
The Law	136
The Royals	137

Entertainment   139
Theater   139
Food and Drink   140
Pubs   140
Restaurants   143
Tea   148
Shopping   149
Important Addresses & Phone Numbers   154

Acknowledgments

My heartfelt thanks to my son Josh whose advice aided in the selection of our Pentium® computer; and to my husband, Jerry, who wrestled into submission the "computerese" connected with the enormous capabilities of the programs needed to put the following work into publishable form.

Introduction

One of the pleasures of traveling in Great Britain is that we share a common language; but the word **"common"** is deceptive because American and British versions of the English language have been diverging ever since Webster put together his *An American Dictionary of the English Language* (1828). When one adds to this, the numerous regional idioms that have developed on both sides of the Atlantic, it can make for difficulties in communication in particular situations.

You need not be concerned, however, about being misunderstood, but there will be times when you may wonder about your hearing as what you are being told sounds right *but not exactly right*. For example, the British say **storm in a teacup,** Americans say *tempest in a teapot*. The British **get dog sick,** leave **footmarks** and they wouldn't touch some things with a **barge pole.** Americans *get sick as a dog,* leave *footprints* and wouldn't touch some things with a *ten-foot pole.*

The British also have many logical and descriptive names for objects but not the ones Americans use, for example: **glove puppet** for *hand puppet,* **fruit machine** for *slot machine*, **Interval** for *Intermission* and **bird table** for *bird feeder*. These do not present problems. The one's that could be troublesome are the words we both use but with completely different meanings, as for example, **homely** to the British pertains to the home, meaning something friendly and comfortable while Americans use *homely* to describe a person considered to be plain. To the British: **graft** is hard work, a **jumper** is a pullover and **half and half** is half porter, half ale. To Americans, *graft* is illicit profits; a *jumper* is a one-piece sleeveless dress and *half and half* is half milk-half cream. Like Americans, the British use different parts of their anatomies to describe how they feel. When frightened, **their hearts go into their boots** while American hearts *go into their mouths*. When over busy, the British **are up to their eyes in work,** Americans are *up to their ears in work.* To make a point, the British **would eat their boots if it isn't so;** Americans *would eat their hats;* and the **British can get to places in two shakes of a duck's whisker,** while for Americans it takes *two shakes of a lamb's tail.*

It should be understood, however, that the Standard English taught in both our school systems is essentially the same, except for differences in pronunciation and spelling. Where this dictionary will help is with everyday words and phrases covering many aspects of British life, together with a liberal sprinkling of words and expressions that can be so puzzling in those delightful British mysteries.

Please note: The official name of Great Britain is **"The United Kingdom of Great Britain and Northern Ireland;" "The UK"** for short.

How To Use This Book

There are two sections to this book: the Dictionary and the Phrasebook. The Dictionary will help you to quickly find the meanings of words and phrases that you may encounter on your trip with the exception of those connected with architecture and archaeology, restaurants, pub offerings, driving, crime and the police. These are listed alphabetically in the Phrasebook together with other useful words connected with specific travel situations such as: accommodations, currency, telephone, shopping, money, weather and the like. Both dictionaries have the same set-up, as for example:

griff scoop *(information)* Give me the scoop.

The British or American word or expression is in bold type, the American or British equivalent follows in plain type. When necessary, for clarification, there will be an explanation *italicized in parentheses,* or a sentence in plain type, or both.

DISCLAIMER

Great pains have been taken to corroborate the facts in this book; however, inevitably errors may occur. Readers are advised that these are times of rapid change. So many varied factors can influence the travel industry and can make up-to-date information change right after publication. Neither the author nor the publisher should be held responsible for any changes that are encountered but we would appreciate being apprised of them for future editions of this book.

Prepare: *from the Latin "praeparare:"*
prae (before), parare (get ready)

Travel Tips

The most important advice I can give to readers of this book is **"prepare."** For example, having boned up on Stonehenge, I will never forget my excitement on seeing it appear on the horizon and grow larger and larger as we approached Wiltshire's, Salisbury Plain. It was like reaching across the centuries to the Bronze Age to touch the minds of those so-called primitive peoples who, using hand tools, displayed a great sophistication in bringing an idea into being. It mattered not that the stones they wanted for their monument were not available locally; they managed to locate and transport the right ones from a distance of 30 miles; and topping that stupendous feat, they transported 80 more, the "bluestones" which weigh up to 4 tons each, from Dyfed, Wales, a distance of 385 km (240 miles). How, no one knows to this day. Then came the job of dressing the stones and erecting them in such a manner that the axis was aligned with the sunrise on June 21st, the longest day of the year. It was the **"praeparare"** that made that experience more meaningful to me.

Herewith, some travel tips to make your holiday experiences as memorable as mine:

1. BONE UP ON THE PLACES YOU INTEND TO VISIT: The 914.3 section of your local library is chock full of books on Britain; and computer buffs can get software versions of familiar travel guides which provide users with maps of popular cities and information on their hotels, restaurants and attractions. Also, programs like Internet, OnLine America, Compuserve and the like provide direct correspondence with fellow Anglophiles or even the Brits themselves.

2. MONEY SAVERS: The British Government created the **British Tourist Authority (BTA)** in 1969 to promote tourism and it has been busy ever since grinding out brochures, maps and pamphlets on every aspect of British life. **"Britain, Your Vacation Planner,"** is an especially useful booklet as it provides a brief overview of the attractions of Britain and, very important, it contains information on a number of money savers **that must be bought in the U.S. before you get on that plane, namely: The BritRail Pass, UK AirPass and Visitor TravelCard**. (BTA, 551 Fifth Avenue, New York, N.Y. 10176-0799. $2.50) Ask also for information on the **Great British Heritage Pass** which allows entry into hundreds of historic properties and gardens, the **London Travel Card** which allows unlimited travel on London buses and subway and the **London for Less** discount card, which allows discounts at over 200 places.

3. ATM'S: Getting cash is easier and faster than cashing traveler's checks in the UK because ATM's (Automatic Teller Machines) are becoming prevalent. Check with your bank and credit card companies regarding whether you can avail yourself of their services there. Also, it would be helpful if you had about **$35 worth of British coins** with you when you arrive in the UK for phone calls, tips, etc. British money can be purchased at many US banks or airport money exchange booths. (See **"Currency"** in the Phrasebook.)

3. DRIVING: If you plan to drive in the UK: check with your insurer or credit card company regarding a collision/damage waiver; also, check with your automobile association to learn whether it has reciprocity arrangements with the UK's AA (Automobile Club) or RAC (Royal Automobile Club).

4. PRESCRIPTION DRUGS: Take enough to last the trip in in your pocket or purse in their original packages; plus a doctor's prescription using the generic name.

5. HOW TO HANDLE DIFFICULTIES:
The U.S. Embassy, London, 24-31 Grosvenor Square, London W1A 1AE, is your first line of defence: **Phone: 44-0171-499-9000; Fax: 44-0171-495-5012.**
— They will replace a lost or stolen passport but you must have ready a police report and proof of citizenship.
— If your money is stolen, you will be helped to contact relatives or friends who can send you money via the consulate; or they'll put you in touch with local groups who assist travelers.

— If you have no way home, they will buy you an airline ticket for a promissory note. Your passport will be restricted until you pay for the ticket.

— In case of illness, doctors and hospitals will be recommended.

— If you are jailed for any reason, someone from the Consular office will visit you to see that you are in good health and are being fed properly. You will be advised regarding your rights and will be given a list of lawyers. The Consulate cannot interfere with the British legal process but will continue to be in touch with you until your case is resolved.

6. WHEN YOUR PLANS ARE COMPLETE:

— Make three copies of your plane tickets, credit cards, driver's license and your passport title page. Be sure to include the following plane reservation information:

Date leaving ....**Date returning**............
Airport.....................**Airport**.........................
Terminal..................**Terminal**......................
Check-in time..........**Check-in time**...............
Flight No...................**Flight No**......................
Flight time................**Flight time**....................
Arrival time.............**Arrival time**.................

— Keep one in your pocket or purse, one in your luggage and give one to a relative at home.

7. FINAL TIP: Just in case your return is delayed for whatever reason, to keep your relatives from worrying, especially Mom and Dad, leave these numbers with them:

Citizen's Emergency Center
Washington, D.C. (1-202-647-5225)
This is a 24-hour travel advisory hotline. Have ready the missing person's name and itinerary.
U.S. Embassy, London, (011-44-0171-499-9000).
Bon Voyage

Five-Minute History of the UK

6000-3000 BC Neolithic Period (New Stone Age)
3000-1500 BC Bronze Age
1500-43 AD Iron Age
43-400 The Roman Period: Celtic Queen Boadicea and her army fight the Romans; Hadrian's Wall is built.
400 The Celts arrive and settle in Ireland, Scotland, Wales and Cornwall; Roman power dwindles.
450-871 Angles, Saxons and Jutes arrive; King Offa builds his Dike; legend of King Arthur has its start.
871-850 Teutons drive Britons to the west.
850 to 1066 Northmen arrive; are fought by Alfred the Great, who is succeeded by Edward, the Confessor, who starts the building of Westminster Abbey; then Harold, Earl of Wessex who is opposed by William, Duke of Normandy. They battle and Harold dies in the Battle of Hastings.
1066-1154 The Normans: William, the Conqueror rules; son, William II, succeeds; followed by brother Henry I; Stephen, Wm. I's grandson; and Henry I's grandson, Henry II.
1154-1399 AD The Plantaganets: Henry II rules England, parts of Ireland and Wales, and France's Normandy, Maine, Anjou, Touraine and Acquitaine; Thomas a'Becket is murdered; Henry's sons succeed: first, Richard, the Lionhearted; then John I, who signs the Magna Carta marking the beginnings of Parliament; son, Henry III succeeds, Baron's War breaks out, Henry III gives Parliament more control; son, Edward succeeds, conquers Wales, declares son Prince of Wales; son becomes Edward II, wars with Scotland, is defeated at Bannockburn and is deposed in favor of son, Edward III; 100-year war with France begins; Black Death kills 1/4 of the people; grandson Richard II succeeds, wants absolute rule, is forced to abdicate and is imprisoned after a revolt by his cousin, Henry of Lancaster.

1399-1461 House of Lancaster: Henry becomes Henry IV; son, Henry V succeeds, renews 100-year war with France, wins battle at Agincourt and dies; son, Henry VI is king at age 9 months and his uncles rule; Joan of Arc inspires French to re-capture their lands; 100-year war ends and War of the Roses begins; Richard of York (White Rose) wants the crown and fights Henry (Red Rose); Richard's son, Edward defeats Henry and places him in the Tower.

1461-1603 House of York: Edward becomes Edward IV; his two sons are placed in the Tower and disappear; Edward's brother, Richard III, succeeds, is opposed by Henry Tudor and is killed at the Battle of Bosworth.

1485-1603 House of Tudor: Henry becomes Henry VII; ends War of Roses by marrying the daughter of Edward IV; son Henry VIII succeeds, cuts ties with Rome when not allowed to divorce Catherine of Aragon; dissolves the marriage himself and marries six women in succession; beheads two and divorces three; is succeeded by son, Edward IV, who is followed by the 9-day Queen, Lady Jane Grey, who is deposed and executed by Henry VIII's daughter Mary I; succeeded by her sister Elizabeth I, who executes Mary, Queen of Scots. It's the time of the Renaissance, Shakespeare and the defeat of the Spanish Armada. Having no issue, Elizabeth appoints James I, the Scottish Queen's son, as her successor.

1603-1714 House of Stuart: James I declares the divine right of kings; son, Charles I succeeds, declares war on Parliament; Civil War erupts; Charles is defeated by Cromwell and is beheaded; England becomes a Commonwealth and later a Protectorate with Cromwell as Lord Protector; his son Richard succeeds and resigns. Parliament offers the crown to Charles I's son; who becomes Charles II; Habeas Corpus Act is passed; the London Plague kills 100,000; the Great fire devastates London; Charles dissolves Parliament; political parties are formed (Tories and Whigs); Catholic brother James II succeeds and is deposed by Parliament in favor of his half-sister Mary and husband William of Orange; they sign the famous Bill of Rights; Queen Anne, Mary's sister succeeds; her Catholic brother, James Stuart becomes the Old Pretender; his son, Bonnie Prince Charlie, fights for the throne but is defeated at Colloden; England and Scotland unite as Great Britain with the Union Jack as the national flag; George I, a German prince and great grandson of James I, succeeds.

1714-1910 House of Hanover: George I only speaks German; leaves the governing to Prime Minister, Robert Walpole; the Industrial Revolution begins; succeeded by son, George II, who leaves governing to Walpole and William Pitt; George III succeeds and loses the American Colonies; Act of Union joins Ireland to England and Britain becomes The United Kingdom of Britain and Northern Ireland; George IV follows; Catholic Emancipation Act is passed; Wm. IV is next; Great Reform Bill is passed; Queen Victoria succeeds; Crimean War, Indian Mutiny, Ireland fights for Home Rule, The Boer War; Edward VII succeeds; helps form Triple Entente of Britain, France and Russia.

1910 to Present House of Windsor: George V succeeds, cuts ties with the Hanoverians when WWI begins; changes the name of his line to House of Windsor; Lloyd George puts the Government of Ireland Act through Parliament; Edward VIII succeeds and abdicates to marry Mrs. Simpson; George VI succeeds, the new Republic of Ireland is proclaimed in 1949; and in 1952, Elizabeth II becomes queen.

THE UNITED KINGDOM
Regions—Counties—Islands

SCOTLAND
*Capital, Edinburgh

Island Councils:
1 Shetland Islands
2 Orkney Islands
3 Western Isles

Regions:
4 Highland
5 Grampian
6 Tayside
7 Central
8 Fife
9 Lothian
10 Strathclyde
11 Borders
12 Dumfries and Galloway

NORTHERN IRELAND
*Capital, Belfast
13 Londonderry
14 Antrim
15 Tyrone
16 Fermanagh
17 Armagh
18 Down

ENGLAND
*Capital, London
The North:
19 Northumberland
20 Cumbria
21 Tyne and Wear
22 Durham
23 Cleveland
24 North Yorkshire

The North West:
25 Lancashire *(Lancs)*
26 Merseyside
27 Greater Manchester
28 Cheshire

Yorkshire (Yorks) and Humberside:
29 West Yorkshire
30 South Yorkshire
31 Humberside
32 Lincolnshire *(Lincs)*

East Midlands:
33 Derbyshire
34 Nottinghamshire *(Notts)*
35 Leicestershire *(Leics)*

West Midlands
36 Northhamptonshire (Northants)
37 Shropshire (Salop)
38 Staffordshire (Staffs)
39 West Midlands
40 Hereford &Worcestershire(Worcs)
41 Warwickshire

East Anglia
42 Norfolk
43 Suffolk

The South East
44 Cambridgeshire*(Cambs)*
45 Bedfordshire *(Beds)*
46 Oxfordshire *(Oxon)*
47 Buckinghamshire *(Bucks)*
48 Hertfordshire *(Herts)*
49 Essex
50 Berkshire *(Berks)*
51 Greater London
52 Surrey
53 Kent
54 West Sussex
55 East Sussex

The South West
56 Gloucestershire *(Glos)*
57 Avon
58 Wiltshire *(Wilts)*
59 Cornwall
60 Devon
61 Somersetshire
62 Dorset
63 Hampshire *(Hants)*

Wales
*Capital: Cardiff
64 Gwynedd
65 Clwyd
66 Powys
67 Dyfed
68 West Glamorgan
69 Mid Glamorgan
70 South Glamorgan
71 Gwent

ISLANDS
72 Isle of Man
73 Isles of Scilly
74 Isle of Wight
75 Channel Islands

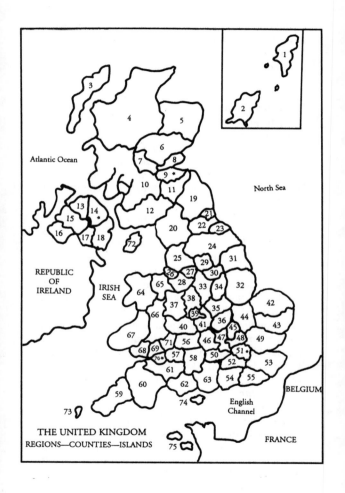

Atlantic Ocean

North Sea

IRISH
SEA

REPUBLIC
OF
IRELAND

BELGIUM

English
Channel

FRANCE

THE UNITED KINGDOM
REGIONS—COUNTIES—ISLANDS

Two-Minute Tour of the UK

Britain may be small but it has such an amazing diversity of landscapes; such a large selection of incredibly interesting historic places and is so chock-full of artifacts **from the year dot** (from the year one), that one can be hard put to decide what to see first. Herewith, a brief review of the attractions in each area:

England's North Country is famous for industry and has many major industrial towns such as Manchester and Liverpool, wonderful countryside, a marvelous network of canals, Neolithic monuments, the Bronte sister's Haworth, a Viking center in York, the famous walled city of Chester, five national parks, the Lake District beloved by Wordsworth and Johnson, the Isle of Man and the Holy Island of Lindesfarne where St. Aidan began to Christianize Britain in the 7th Century.

Central England covers the area from Wales to Norwich and has seen many tragic events connected with its Royals (Market Bosworth and Fotheringhay) and has many of their beautiful homes (Sandringham and Hatfield House). Besides its famous cities and towns (London and Birmingham), it has a literary history (Shakespeare's Stratford-upon-Avon and Robin Hood's Nottingham). It is also the home of Oxford and Cambridge and holds a unique place in history as the birthplace of the Industrial Revolution, when in 1709, Abraham Derby invented the technique of smelting iron ore with coke near Ironbridge Gorge in Shropshire.

Southern England extends from Land's End to the river Thames. It has many places associated with the legendary King Arthur ; as well as Glastonbury, the reputed resting place of the Holy Grail. It also has reminders of prehistory with Stonehenge and Avebury; Roman history with the ruins of Roman baths in Bath; America's beginnings with Plymouth and present history with Windsor, Queen Elizabeth's favorite home.

Wales, though small, has a diversity of landscapes from the rugged mountain peaks and lakes of Snowdonia to the beautiful bays and inlets of the coast. It's very famous for its Eisteddfodau, a yearly international musical festival of Welsh music and literature and Caernarvon Castle where the Princes of Wales are invested.

Scotland, home of tragic Mary, Queen of Scots and her son, James VI, who Elizabeth I named as her successor as James I of England. He was born in Edinburgh (pronounced Edin-borough) Castle. Scotland is also famous for industry; whisky (scotch); John O'Groats, northermost village of Scotland; Ben Nevis, Britain's highest mountain; St. Andrew, home of golf, and Inverness' Loch Ness monster.

Northern Ireland is famous for its Stone Age tombs and Norman Castles. The spectacular stones of the Giant's Causeway are a fascination for thousands of yearly visitors as well as the walkable tops of the massive stone walls of Londonderry. Thousands of pilgrims visit Armagh, the spiritual capital of Ireland and Downpatrick, the grave of St. Patrick, Ireland's patron saint. Belfast, the capital, is a great cultural and industrial center.

BRITISH-AMERICAN DICTIONARY

A to Zed A to Z

absey book primer

absolutely top hole super-duper

acid drop lemon drop

ack-emma and pip-emma A.M. and P.M. *(names devised by British Army signallers)*

ag English *(tennis term, short for "agony;" that is, giving the ball a spin to make it unreturnable)* Put some ag on the ball!

Ah, there you are! Hi, glad to see you!

air jacket May West *(life jacket)*

alamode *(beef that is larded and stewed with vegetables; (US) pie topped with ice cream)*

alarm calls wake up calls *(at a hotel)*

Albert, an *(short watch chain like the one Prince Albert wore)*

all at one go all at once

all the same just the same

alphabet bricks alphabet blocks

altitude nil altitude zero

American cloth, glazed tablecloth oil cloth

anorak parka

anti-clockwise counter-clockwise

Are you black or white? How do you like your coffee? *(With milk or without?)*

argy-bargy fuss

arrested pinched

As if I bloody well cared! As if I gave a hoot!

as like him as she can stare as like him as she can be

as near as dammit as close as can be

as right as a trivet as right as rain

as she comes straight: Want some rum, dash of orange or straight.

ash pan ash tray

Ask me no questions, hear no lies. Ask me no questions, I'll tell you no lies.

assembly-room public ballroom

at cost price at cost

at the head of the poll winner of an election

aubergine, brinjal, egg fruit, brown jolly eggplant

B aby's dummy pacifier

back chat back talk

backacting trencher back hoe

back-kick side effects (*of medicine*)

backalong a while back: I worked with her a while back.

backing-down gold-bricking (*shirking work*)

bad form bad manners

bad lot, a a no good

Bad cess to them! Bad luck to them!

Bad show! Tough going!

bag grab: I'll buy your ticket and grab some seats.

baker's board, moulding board bread board (*for kneading dough*)

baker's shop bakery

balaclavas woolen caps (*name taken from the warm woolen headgear covering the ears and back of the head during the severe cold weather in the Crimean War*)

ball is at one's feet ball is in one's lap (*decision time*)

bang on right on the nose, right on the money, right on target

banker's order bank check

banking account bank account

banknote bill

barmaid, barman bartender

barrier train gate (*at a railroad station*)

base minded dirty minded

bashing squandering: They don't go squandering all their money.

batchy terrible

bath safety rail bathtub security rail

bath-tap bathtub faucet

bath-wrap terry robe

bathroom and lavatory *(usually two separate rooms; the bathroom is for baths and has a tub and washbasin; the lavatory is called the loo or W.C.- Water Closet)*

bathroom basin, washhand basin washbasin, bathroom sink

baths, swimming baths pool, swimming pool

bath bathtub

bathing costume bathing suit, swimsuit

bathroom basin bathroom sink

be a candidate run for office

be darned shot be damned: What women see in him, I'll be damned if I know!

be hard done by be treated badly

be in a bit of a cleft stick be in a bind

be in low water be short *(lacking essential money)*

be lumbered with be saddled with

be on form doing very well

bear a hand give a hand

bear the bell, carry off the bell come in first

beastly weather, filthy weather miserable weather

beastly terrible

beat to sticks beat to the ground

beavered slaved: He slaved at polishing my brass.

bed sitter, combined room studio apartment

Beetle off! Stuff it! Push off! Cut it out! Knock it off!

beetled rushed: He rushed off.

beetroot beets

bespoke suit, hand-cut suit custom made suit

Best of British luck! Good luck! *("Best of British," without "luck" is usually satirical.)*

between two lights *(under cover of darkness)*

betty, a a man who does woman's work

bicycle bin bicycle basket

bicycle lamp bicycle headlight

big pot, a a big shot *(a show off)*

billycock fedora *(man's hat)*

bird table bird feeder

bird-witted dimwitted

bird chick *(slang for "young woman")*

Birthday Honours *(honours, titles such as Sir, etc., granted on the monarch's birthday)*

biscuit packet cookie box

biscuit (sweet) cookie

biscuit (savoury) cracker

black as ink black as coal

black in the face blue in the face

blackleg strike breaker

Blimey! Goodness!

bloody awful terrible

bloody awkward patch, a bad spot: We may be in a bad spot.

bloody marvelous fantastic: It was a fantastic way to let off steam.

bloody stupid damned dumb: Don't be so damned dumb!

blooming miserable: It's a miserable waste of energy!

blower horn *(slang for telephone)*

Blue Book *(parliamentary publication with a blue cover; (US) a social register)*

boards, the the stage

bobby dazzler a great soccer player *(soccer is called "football" in the UK)*

bobby-horse hobby-horse *(a horse on a merry-go-round)*

bog, loo the john *(a toilet)*

bomb, a *(an excellent play (US) a failure)*

boob make a booboo: Did I make a booboo?

book-account *(an account of debt or credit in a bankbook)*

book-post book mailing

booking-board reservations list

booking-clerk ticket seller

booking office ticket office

book tally, book token book gift certificate

boot-button eyes shoe button eyes

bootlace tie string tie

bootlace shoelace, shoestring

bored rigid bored stiff

bore gauge: He used a 12 gauge shotgun.

bottle party BYOB party *(Bring Your Own Booze party)*

bottle-slider *(tray for passing a decanter round the table)*

bounder cad

braces suspenders

brackets parenthesis

bread corn wheat

break a lance with enter into a contest with

break-up school vacation

breast the tape break the tape *(touching the stretched line at the end of a foot race)*

brekker breakfast

brick-tea *(tea pressed into bricks)*

brimstone and treacle sulphur and molasses

British plate German silver

brolly bumbershoot *(umbrella)*

Buck House *(Buckingham Palace)*

buckwheat *(used in Europe as feed for horses cattle and poultry; (US) ground into flour for pancakes called "buckwheats.")*

Building Society Savings and Loan Bank

build-up trays stacking trays *(in an office)*

bullion van armored car

bullock's heart papaw

bullyrag badger

bum-freezer *(slang for a short evening jacket)*

bumping race *(race where boats bump each other)*

bunch of fives knuckle sandwich *(the fist)*

bun sweet roll

burning glass magnifying glass

bush telegraph, the the grapevine *(slang for gossip)*

busman bus driver
butter boat (*pot holding melted butter*)
butterine (*margarine made partly from milk*)
butter muslin cheesecloth
buttery wine storeroom
buttonhole boutonniere

C.A., Chartered Accountant CPA, Certified
Public Accountant

C.P., Clerk of the peace JP, Justice of the Peace
cabbage, to to purloin
cadge a lift to hook a ride
cake cookie, sweet roll
call over the coals, haul over the coals rake over
the coals
camelcloth coat camel hair coat
cami-knicker teddy, teddy briefer
campion pinks
can't make tops or bottoms of it can't make heads
or tails of it
can't stick it can't take it
capital murder capital offense
Capital! Great!
capsicum peppers
careers master guidance counselor
carriage forward payment on delivery
carriage-paid prepaid delivery
carried the can was a patsy
**cashiered, sacked, got one's cards, got the books,
got to the wall, got the bucket** let go, got the ax,
was fired
cash on the nail cash on the barrelhead
cast one's water urinalysis
caster sugar granulated sugar
Casualty Ward Accident Ward
catapult slingshot
catch a lift hitchhike
cat's mustache, the the cat's meow

chair organ choir organ

chamber fellow school roommate

chance-found found by chance

changing room locker room

chapel master music director, conductor

charabanc, tourist bus tour bus

charley, a (*short triangular beard like that of Charles I*)

chat up get to know: You should get to know that new girl.

chatting acquaintance nodding acquaintance

checquebook checkbook

checque check

cheek nerve: She has a lot of nerve to come to you about this.

Cheers! Bottoms up!

Cheery-o! Cheery bye! So long! Bye Bye!

cheeseparing cost cutting

Chemist Drugstore

cherry fizz cherry soda

chew the cud chew the fat

chicory endive

chimney pot hat top hat

chine of beef rib roast

chippy (*fish and chips shop; (US) prostitute*)

chips (*french fries; (US) potato chips*)

chivvied bounced around: We were bounced around from camp to camp.

chuck up throw up

chucker-out bouncer

chunter chatter

church rate weekly offering

Church Army Salvation Army

Church Parade Easter Parade (*fashion parade after Easter services*)

cinema, the pictures movies

cistern, flush box toilet tank

City Guarantee Society Bankers Insurance Company

clamper botch up

clanger boner *(faux pas)*

clay pigeon shooting trap shooting

clean as a new pin clean as a pin

clean someone's clock punch someone in the face

Clearing Banks Bank Clearing Houses

clever dicks smart alecs

cleverer than one looks smarter than one looks

Cloak Room Rest Room

cloakroom ticket baggage check

Clock Golf *(putting game on a green marked like a clock dial in which the player putts from each hour-figure to a hole near the center)*

close cul-de-sac

close time closed season *(illegal hunting season)*

close-stool commode

clothespeg clothespin

co-op foodhall co-op market

coach bus

cobs of maize corncobs

cock-a-hoop, over the moon, in high feather pleased as punch: You must have been pleased as punch on getting that raise.

cocked snooks thumbed one's nose

coffee morning coffee klatch

cold house cold frame

collar stiffener collar stay

collected gathered up: She gathered up the cups.

collection bag collection box *(in a church)*

college cap mortar board

colour washing water paint

come over queer feel wierd suddenly

come the innocent play the innocent

comedy chat comedy routine

comic turn comic act

comings in, the income

commercial room *(hotel room set aside for commercial travelers)*

Committee on Safety of Medicines Food and Drug Administration, FDA

Commissioner For Oaths Notary Public

Common Ward Ward (*of a hospital*)

conchie conscientious

constituency voting district

constituents voters

cook-shop restaurant

cooker stove

cookery book cookbook

cooking chocolate baking chocolate

copped a basinful had it: Your brother looks as if he's had it.

copped caught, arrested

coppice small grove of trees

corgettes zucchini, squash

cork drip-mat coaster

corn flour (*finely ground maize, rice or other grain*)

cornet ice cream cone

corn flags gladiolas

cornflour cornstarch

corn grain of any kind

cost a packet cost an arm and a leg: His boat must have cost an arm and a leg.

cost-free, free cost free of charge

cost-sale house wholesale firm

costermonger's cart fruit peddler's truck

costing meeting financial meeting: I have a long financial meeting this morning..

cottage loaf (*loaf of bread that resembles a small loaf sitting atop a large loaf*)

cotton reel spool of thread

cotton wool cotton

cough sweets, throat pastilles cough drops

council school public school

counter clerk teller, bank clerk

counter foil ticket stub

country baps (*rolls resembling hamburger buns*)

County Town County Seat

coupe' (*half compartment on British railroad cars*)

courgettes, marrow, vegetable marrow zucchini, squash

court shoes pumps

coverts thickets

cow gum rubber cement

cow heel *(ox-foot stewed to a jelly)*

cowardly custard chicken or yellow

Cox's orange pippin *(eating apple)*

cracking perfect: It's a perfect day!

crack-jaw jaw breaker *(word that's difficult to pronounce)*

crackling dottle drivel

crafty 48, a *(British army term for two days leave)*

crash tender emergency truck

crashing howlers bad mistakes *(in grammar)*

crazy paving flagstone walk

crinkly, the paper money

crisps potato chips

croaker, a a killer

crockery dishes

crocodile-skin handbag alligator bag

cross-grained crabby

cross-head screwdriver Phillips screwdriver

cross-sill sleeping car *(on a train)*

crummy *(cow with a crumpled horn; (US) cheap or miserable)*

crumpet English muffin

cruncher, the the punchline

cup-tie *(one of a series of games to determine the winners of a cup)*

cupman drinking buddy

cups *(various summer drinks containing alcohol diluted with water)*

current account checking account

curriculum vitae school transcript

curtain-up curtain time *(in a theatre)*

cushy number easy job

cut-price wine shops cut-rate liquor stores

cut-throat razor straight razor

cutting by cutting ahead *(of another car)*

Dabs fingerprints

dabster expert: When it came to making something out of nothing, he was an expert.

damn box-up damned foul-up: The whole thing was a damned foul-up.

darbies hand cuffs

dashed clever darned clever

dead latches dead bolts

dead meat *(meat ready for market)*

dead men *(empty bottles after a carouse)*

dead men's bells foxglove

deaf aid hearing aid

decent sort a good fellow

decent tea *(one with lots of food)*

deepie 3-D movie

dekko, a a look: Let's have a look at her.

Delinquent Notice Overdraft

demerara sugar brown sugar

desk porter desk clerk

devilling research: Can you do a bit of research for me?

dextrose made from maize corn-sugar

dialling tone dial tone

dicey chancey

dickey rumble seat *(on a car)*

digestive biscuits graham crackers

digs furnished apartments, houses

Dining Hall Lunch Room *(in a school)*

dinner gong dinner bell

Directory Inquiries Telephone Book

Disabled Soldiers Institute Veterans Hospital

dish of tea cup of tea

dished dumped: She was very happy she had dumped him.

dishy foxy *(glamourous)*

diving kit diving gear

do affair: I'm going to the charity affair.

doctor's stuff medicine

doctor's tackle doctor's black bag

dodges tricks: He's up to all sorts of tricks.

dog kennel cubby hole *(tiny office)*

dog sick sick as a dog

Dog's chance! Fat chance!

doing a locum *(substituting for a doctor or minister)*

doing sweet all doing nothing

dolly-catch *(an easy catch)*

Don't gnaw more than you can chomp. Don't bite off more than you can chew.

Don't muck about! Don't mess around!

donkey food bran *(bran breakfast cereal)*

Don *(a Fellow in a college or a college authority)*

doorkeeper doorman

Dorothy bag drawstring bag

double cream heavy cream

double glazing storm windows

Down-Line *(railroad line leading from a town center; an Up-Line does the opposite)*

doyley doiley

draining board drain board

dram drink: Care for a drink?

draper dry goods store

draught excluder weather stripping

draughts checkers

draw cuts cast lots

drawing pins thumb tacks

dressed to the nines, dressed up like a dog's pillow dressed to the teeth, dressed up like the cat's meow

drinks trolley drinks cart

dry file wet blanket, party pooper

drop a clanger, drop a spanner in the works, drop a brick pull a boner, drop a wrench in the works, make a boo-boo

drug-taker drug addict: He's a confirmed drug addict.

duck's egg *(the zero "O" on a scoring sheet which indicates that a player made no runs)*

dudder second hand clothing store

duds *(poor or ragged clothes; (US) clothes of any kind)*

dumb brick dumb bunny

dumb piano soundless keyboard

dust cart garbage truck

dustbin garbage can

Earbob earring

earlap ear muff

earnest money, earnest penny *(a pledge)*

Education Rates School Taxes

egg-glass egg timer

egg-powder powdered eggs

eggbeater chopper *(helicopter)*

eggler butter-and-egg man

Egyptian pea chickpea

eiderdown comforter

elastic knitted textile fabric stockinet

elastoplast, sticking plaster bandaid, adhesive bandage

election agent campaign manager

electiontide election time

electric flex electric cord

emulsion latex paint

enclosed order of nuns cloistered nuns

engaged tone busy signal *(telephone)*

engine driver engineer *(on a railroad)*

enjoying it frightfully having a ball

essence extract

estate agent realtor

evanescent ink, sympathetic ink invisible ink

evenfall dusk

Evergreen Clubs Golden Years Clubs

exchange line telephone

excisement tax collectors

ex-directory unlisted *(telephone)*

exhibitioner scholarship winner

export rejects seconds

express goods fast freight
eye bath eye cup

(Face**)flannel** face cloth

fagged worn out
faggotist bassonist
faggots sausages
fags coffin nails (*cigarettes*)
fairy lights Christmas tree lights
fal-lals doo-dads
family saloon family car
fancy dive swan dive
fancy fair, fete bazaar
fancy goods showy materials
fancy man pimp
fancy woman mistress, prostitute
fast handed close-fisted
favour (*knot of ribbons worn at an election or wedding*)
fed up to the back teeth fed up to the teeth
feeling a bit dicky feeling a bit off the weather
feeling chuft feeling flush (*from receiving lots of money*)
feeling fit feeling ok
financial boffins financial wizards
find one's feet get back on one's feet
fire raising arson: Firemen were standing by in case arson was reported.
Fire ahead! Fire away! Talk!
Fire Brigade Fire Department
first floor (*the floor above the ground floor; (US) the second floor*)
fish and chips twice (*a double order*)
fish cake fish croquette
fish fingers fish sticks
fishmongers fish store
fit as a flea fit as a fiddle
fitted carpet wall-to-wall carpet

Fiver *(five pounds in British money)*

fixture *(an appointment; (US) a wall lamp)*

flag flapper flag waver

flaming good great: That's great!

flapjack *(oatmeal pancake; (US) batter griddlecake or pancake)*

flat apartment

flesh brush back scrubber

flipping a wiper waving a hankie

flipping miserable: It was a miserable debacle.

flogging a dead horse beating a dead horse

flog peddle: He was off to peddle the stuff he'd been stealing.

fly-fisher fly-fisherman

fold-up bed cot

foolscap size letter size

football soccer

footballer soccer player

footmarks footprints

footway path

for a donkey's years for ages

fork supper casserole, one-dish meal

form *(a long seat or a bench; a school class)*

Fours or **Fourses** *(snack taken at four o'clock)*

foxed looped *(drunk)*

freak-peeps freak shows *(at a fair)*

free fisher *(one who has permission to fish in certain waters)*

free list complimentary ticket list *(list of persons admitted free to a theatre)*

free pub *(a pub that offers many brands of beer; "tied pubs" sell only one brand being tied, so to speak, to one producer)*

french-bean kidney bean , butter bean

French plum prune

French bed day bed

fresher freshman

frightfully brilliant brainy

frock dress

frogman suit wetsuit

froth-blower *(beer drinker)*

fruit gum machine chewing gum machine

fruit jellies jello

fruit machine slot machine

fruit pastilles gum drops

full academicals cap and gown

full marks excellent, A-plus

full stop period

fully qualified graduated

fun arcades penny arcades

funk-hole escape hatch: It was an escape hatch used for quick getaways.

Furnished Show Flat Model apartment

furniture van, pantechnicon, removal van moving van, furniture truck

G**ames master, games mistress** physical education instructor

games tunics gym suits

gamey leg game leg

gammon ham

gang-breaker gangbuster

gangways theater aisles: At intermission, the people began to stream into the theater aisles and lobby.

gaspers *(cheap cigarettes)*

Gaudy Day and Gaudy Night *(annual college festival)*

gaufer-stitched smocks ruffled smocks, fluted smocks

gazogene carbonator *(apparatus for making aerated water)*

general stores staples: He went to buy vegetables and some staples.

gent's cycle man's bicycle

gent's hair dresser barber

Gentlemen of the Privy Chamber *(officials in the royal household who are in attendance at court)*

genuine real, on the up and up

get into ceremonial get dressed up

get one's monkey up, have one's monkey up get one's dander up

get shot of someone get rid of someone

get the wrong end of the stick get the dirty end of the stick

Get cracking! Get weaving! Get going!

getting past it nearing retirement: He was nearing retirement anyway.

getting under one's wool getting under one's skin

gets beet red, assumes a prawn-like hue blushes

giglamps, spectacles glasses (*eye glasses*)

giggle a little joke: It was a little joke.

gilet vest

ginger-nut (*small thick gingersnap*)

ginger pop, gingerade gingerale

gingerbread biscuit gingersnap

give one the toe of one's boot give one the boot

give one's ears for something give one's eyes for something (*to want something badly*)

Give it a miss! Skip it!

glass of bubbly (*a drink*)

glove puppet hand puppet

go bonkers, go round the twist go bananas, go round the bend

go brown get tan

go off at half cock go off half-cocked

go over with a swing go over with a bang

go poopsie go haywire: Why did everything she touched go haywire?

gob-stoppers candy (*"gob" is slang for "mouth"*)

goer go-getter

God Save the Queen Good Night Sweetheart (*usually played at the end of a dance or ball*)

going full belt, going at it hammer and tongs going full steam ahead

going up the spout going under (*a failing as a failing business*)

going up (*going to a university*)

golf trolley golf cart
gone missing missing: She's missing again!
Good-oh! Great!
goods station freight station
goods trains, goods-waggons freight trains
gooseberry, a a fifth wheel
got up to kill dressed to kill
grass mowings grass clippings
grass, sparrow grass asparagus
grateful for small mercy grateful for small favors
greatcoat overcoat
green fingers green thumbs
green room dressing room (*traditional name for actor's dressing rooms, no matter what color, because originally dressing rooms had green walls*)
gridiron, teakettle railroad
griff scoop (*information*) Give me the scoop.
grill broiler
Grit your teeth and soldier on. Grin and bear it!
grumble, a a gripe
guernsey (*close-fitting knitted sweater worn by sailors*)
gumboots rubbers
gymkhana athletic event (*meeting or show with horse contests*)

H

Ha-ha (*sunken ditch edging a park or garden*)
hacking jacket riding jacket
hackney carriages taxis (*London's famous black taxis*)
hag-ridden scared to death
hair grips bobby pins
hair slide hair clip
half-hunter (*watch whose face is protected by a metal case*)
half-seas over soused
half-term mid-term

half-timbered (*buildings having walls with wooden frames and brick or plaster fillings*)

half-wellingtons (*short, close-fitting rubber boots that are worn under trousers*)

Half a mo! Half a tick! Just a sec!

hand's turn, a a bit of work: He's never done a bit of work in his life.

hard boys toughs

hard cheese tough deal (*a difficult situation*) I think it's tough deal for Tony.

hard sweet hard candy, jawbreaker

Hard graft! Tough going! Too bad!

haricots dried beans

Hark at him! Look at him!

hate their entrails hate their guts

have a bee in one's trousers have a bee in one's bonnet

have a long purse have lots of money, loaded

have one on put one on

have one's heart in one's boots have one's heart in one's mouth (*when frightened*)

have the black ox tread on one's foot going through a bad period

have the key of the street homeless

Have a chair. Have a seat.

haversack backpack

having a mother and father of a row having a grandfather of a fight

haymaker (*country dance; (US) a powerful punch with a fist*)

He's a daisy! He's a dilly!

head hugger kerchief

headlamp headlight

headmaster/headmistress school principal

health lamp heat lamp

hedge buying hedging (*in a stock market*)

hedge marriage secret marriage

heeled (*having a gun; (US) "wealthy"*)

hessian sacking, crocus sacks burlap bags

Hi old thing! Hi funny face! (*terms of endearment*)

high board diving board

high-fed pampered

high-low *(high shoe fastened in front)*

high table *(the Don's table in a college dining-hall)*

high-tasted *(having a strong piquant taste)*

high tea *(a meal with meats etc. as opposed to "plain tea")*

hire charge rental

hive honey honey

hoax calls false alarms

hobjobber, casual odd jobs man

hoky-poky, hokey-pokey *(a kind of ice cream sold on the streets)*

holdall shopping bag

Hold on. Hang on. *(telephone expression)*

Hold your jaw! Keep your trap shut!

hole in one's coat stain on one's reputation

home and dry homefree

home-and-home *(games played alternately on different home grounds)*

home-keeping housekeeping

homefelt heartfelt

homely *(pertaining to the home, familiar; (US) plain or ugly)*

hooted tooted: The car tooted.

hoover vacuum cleaner *(generic in the UK for all vacuum cleaners)*

horse-box *(railroad car for horses, a shipboard stall or a high-sided church pew)*

horse races *(The five chief British annual horse-races are: (1) The Two Thousand Guineas, (2) The One Thousand, (3) The Derby, (4) The Oaks and (5) The St. Leger.)*

horse riding horseback riding

hosepipe garden hose

hotchpotch hodgepodge

hot-and-hot *(food cooked and served up at once in hot dishes)*

hot dog sausage sandwich frankfurter, hot dog

hot-gospeller revivalist preacher
hotel attendant bell-boy
house tax, house duty real estate tax
household franchise, household suffrage universal
   suffrage
household pins straight pins
Household Troops (*Guards Regiments whose
   particular duty is to attend the sovereign and
   defend the metropolis*)
housewife sewing kit *(pocket sewing outfit)*
Housey Housey Bingo
How ghastly! How awful!
human oyster close-mouthed individual: He's very
   close-mouthed.
hundreds-and-thousands sprinkles *tiny candies
   used as ornamental dressing on cakes and biscuits*)
hunting mass (*abridged mass for impatient hunters*)
hunting-tide (*hunting season*)
hunt the gowk a fool's errand
hush line hot line

I have a crow to pick with you. I have a bone to
   pick with you.
I must be toddling along. I must be going.
I say! Hey!
I take your point. I get the point.
I'll eat my boots if it isn't so. I'll eat my hat if it isn't
   so.
I'm extremely sorry. I'm very sorry.
I'm no end obliged. I owe you.
ice pail ice bucket
iced lager cold beer
icing sugar confectioner's sugar
identity bracelet identification bracelet
in a muck sweat in a hurry
in a tick in a minute
in bother, in the cart in trouble
in clobber dressed

in date order in chronological order

in fighting fit, in the pink of health in good shape,
   in the pink

in future from now on

in pod, preggers, preggio pregnant

in the cart out of business *(business failure)*

in the fullness of time in due time

in the pink, starkers birthday suit

in two shakes of a duck's whisker in two shakes of a
   duck's tail

in two ticks, in two two's in a sec

in weal and woe through thick and thin

india-rubber boots rubber boots

ink slinger writer

inland revenue duty income tax

Inland Revenue Internal Revenue Service, IRS

innocent as a babe unborn innocent as a newborn
   babe

Inquiry Agent Detective, P.I. (Private Investigator)

Instrument Out of Order Phone Out of Order *(sign)*

insurance scheme insurance plan

Interval Intermission (*at a theatre*)

invalid chair, Bath chair wheel chair

inverted commas quotation marks

investment firm subscribers investors

invigilator proctor

ironmonger hardware store

It pongs! Now, I remember!

It's fixed! It's a date!

It's the real McKay! It's the real McCoy!

ivy English ivy

Jack towel roller towel

jam doughnut jelly doughnut

jam roll jelly roll

jankers detention *(in school or the army)*

japanned leather patent leather

jape joke: They couldn't see what a joke it was.

jar stein *(of beer)*

Jaw Factory on the Thames Foggy Bottom *(slang names for Parliament and Washington, D.C.)*

jelly gelatin

jersey sweater

jiggery-pokery hocus-pocus

Job's news bad news

John apple, apple-John *(variety of apple considered to be in perfection when shrivelled and withered)*

joint and two veg type meat and potatoes type

joint first tied in first place *(sports expression)*

joke drawings cartoons

jolly rum very unusual: It's very unusual, isn't it?

jolly shambles, a mug's business a mess

Jolly decent! Jolly good show! Fine! Great! Wonderful!

jot bit: There's no evidence for or against his story. Not one solitary bit!

jumble sale rummage sale

jumpers and trousers sweaters and slacks

jumper pullover

Juvenile Hall Reform School

Kack-handed, cack-handed clumsy

keen as mustard sharp as a tack

keenest rates lowest rates *(on bank loans)*

keep a term regular attendance *(at a school or university)*

keep one's eyes skinned keep one's eyes peeled

kentish cobs hazel nuts, filberts

kerb drill fire drill

kerfuffle nonsense: You took a lot of nonsense from Jim.

key fob key holder

kickup *(a dance)*

kick up a fuss, a dust, a row make a fuss

kiosk booth

kip chow down

kipping napping, eating

kipskin calfskin

kiss the rod *(submit to punishment)*

kissing comfit breath mint

kissing-crust *(while baking, the part of the top crust of a loaf of bread which overhangs and touches another)*

kitchen paper paper towels

kit oneself outfit oneself

kite plane *(aeroplane)*

kiting kite flying

knackered exhausted

knackers castanets, clappers

knickerbockers knickers ~~knickers type of women's underpants~~

knob of butter lump of butter

knock up to score having a number of runs *(in a game)*

knock up *(to rouse someone by knocking on a door; (US) to get with child)*

knocked sideways knocked for a loop: She had a smile that knocked him for a loop.

knocked up knocked out *(exhausted)*

Labour Exchange Unemployment Office

Ladies' Gallery *(a gallery in the House of Commons)*

ladies' cycle girl's bicycle

ladies' purse notecase ladies' wallet

laminate formica

lamp standard lamppost

larder pantry

last Monday week a week ago last Monday

last trump Doomsday

Last Unction Extreme Unction *(the last rites of the Catholic Church)*

lavatory paper, loo paper toilet tissue, toilet paper

lay on tea serve tea

layabouts lazybones, lazy louts

laying table setting the table: How about setting the table for me?

laughing academy booby hatch

leadfoil wrapping aluminum foil

leading coach first car *(of a train)*

leathers chamois

leaving shop pawnshop

leaving students, school leavers seniors, graduates

Left-Luggage Office, Lost Property Office Lost & Found, Baggage Office

legged it hotfoot hotfooted it: He hotfooted it for Brussels.

lemon squash lemon soda

letter box, post box mail box

Let's return to our muttons. Let's get back to the subject. *(from an old French farce in which the witnesses kept straying away from the subject-sheep-until the judge in exasperation exclaimed, "Ravenons a nos moutons.")*

Licensed Family Hotel *(hotel with a liquor license)*

Licensee: *(pub owner)*

lickspittle, pushful peeler bootlicker, apple polisher

life peer *(peer whose title is not hereditary but only his for his own lifetime)*

liftman elevator operator

lifts elevators

light fittings light fixtures

like a clock like clockwork

like a kick in the head like a kick in the teeth

like a sack of coals like a ton of bricks

Like boggery! Like fun!

like dust rotten *(contemptible)*

like houses on fire like a house on fire

like living in a shop window like living in a goldfish bowl

linen basket bread basket *(referring to the belly area of the body)*

linen hamper, linen bin clothes hamper

ling codfish, heather

lino linoleum

live box *(box for live fish)*
liver sausage liverwurst
Local, The *(the local pub)*
lodger renter
loft attic
lolly cash, moola *(a percentage of the take)*
London pea-souper London fog
long figure high price
long home the grave
long purples purple loosestrife *(purple wildflowers)*
looking like a thousand pounds, looking like 30 shillings in the pound looking like a million
Lord's table communion rail
Lord's *(famous London cricket ground)*
Lords and Ladies of the Bedchamber *(officers of the royal household who wait in turn upon a king or queen)*
lorry truck
lot of madam load of bull...: That's a load of bull...!
Love Monger Lonely Hearts Club
lucifer match
luck-penny *(a penny returned for good luck by a seller)*
luggage trolleys luggage carts
Luggage Room Check Room *(at a railroad station)*
lumber room storage room, junk room

Mac, mack, mackintosh raincoat

maffick, mafficking *(celebrating exultingly as the British did in London after the relief of the town of Mafeking South Africa on May 17, 1900)*
Many happy returns! Happy birthday! *(Usually said to adults; "Happy birthday." is for children; it's not normally said to an adult, except as a joke.)*
make a stand take a stand *(to stop and offer resistance)*
making a hole in the water drowning

making ducks and drakes of things making a mess of everything

mardy dopey

marks points *(used for scoring in sports)*

mark with a white stone born with a silver spoon in the mouth *(marked as particularly fortunate)*

mascot charm *(for a bracelet)*

mash spuds *(potatoes)*

matey kissy kissy *(very friendly)*

Matron Head Nurse

mean pinch penny, stingy

Meat brain! Meathead! *(name calling)*

Medical Council Medical Society

megrim migraine

Men & Women's Open Toilets Men & Women's Rest Rooms *(sign)*

mews *(stables converted into flats)*

milk float milk delivery truck

milk run *(milkman's morning round; (US) pilot's routine flight)*

minced meat ground meat

Mind the time! Keep track of the time!

Mind your eye! Take care! Look out!

minikinis bikini panties

Miss Prunes and Prisms Miss Prim

money pusher bank clerk

money-scrivener *(one who does financial business for clients)*

monkey-bag *(small money bag hung around the neck)*

monkey nut peanut

Moses basket portable baby bed

muck sweat awful rush: He was in an awful rush to get there.

mucking about fooling around: He's always fooling around in his little yawl.

mugg up bone up, cram: You don't have to bone up on that stuff.

mug-house, ale house bar

mulligrubs colic, sulkiness: She has the colic.

mutton dummies white sneakers
mutton-ham (*salted leg of mutton*)

N.H.I., National Health Insurance Medicare

naffling raving
nail varnish nail polish
nappies diapers
nark at eat away at (*bother with persistent criticism*)
narked peeved
National Savings Certificates U.S Bonds
nattering chattering: What are you two chattering about in there?
Naughts and Crosses Tick-Tack-Toe
neck or nothing go for broke (*risking everything*)
necklet necklace
Neopolitan ice (*a combination of two different ices*)
never-never, the the installment plan
nervy (*nervous or excited; (US) bold or impudent*)
new milk fresh milk
Newmarket (*a racing town or a close-fitting coat*)
night class night school
nil nothing, zero, zilch: We lost 100 to nothing.
nips like one o'clock zips off in a flash
noises-off sound effects: There were plenty of routine sound effects in this film.
Not and earthly! Not for nuts! Not half! No way! Fat Chance! Not on your life!
Not at all! Forget it! Don't mention it!
note-case wallet
notice board bulletin board
NSOB, Not Sporting Old Bean (*popular expression*)

Oat cake oat cracker

off-the-peg clothes off-the-rack clothes
offscum refuse, garbage
Oh I say! Is that right! How touching!

Oh, Queen Anne's dead! That's old news!

oil around come around: He thought Brown would eventually come around to his apartment.

old banger clunker

Old Blighty Uncle Sam *(affectionate names for Britain and the U.S.)*

Old Fruit, Old mate Old Pal

on strap on the cuff

on the cheap economically

on the trot on the go

on tick on credit, on the cuff

one-off, a *(a happening that one determines not to repeat)*

one's tea is running out one's luck is running out

Open Day Parent's Night *(at a school)*

Opening Time *(the time a pub officially opens)*

Operating Theatre Operating Room

ordinary letter post regular mail

osiers willows

oven gloves oven mitts

overalls smocks

overdated out of date

overshooting overreaching

Oxford bags *(very wide trousers)*

P.O.D., Pay On Delivery C.O.D., Cash On Delivery

packed up, snuffed it, took the ferry, called it a day, went over the rainbow, the big dark, dead as mutton, pegged out, went west kicked the bucket, bought the farm *(death)*

packet, parcel package

packet bundle: It'll cost you a bundle.

palette knife spatula

panti-tights pantyhose

Pantos, Pantomimes *(plays that are usually given at Christmas)*

paraffin kerosene *(US) paraffin is "wax")*

parcelling up groceries bagging groceries
parishes *(slang for salesmen's territories)*
Parliament rises Congress adjourns
pass-out marks final grades
Passing Out Ceremony Graduation Ceremony
paste pie crust dough
Pastry-Cook's Shop Bakery
patty tart
pattern husband ideal husband
pavement, footwalk sidewalk
pay as you earn pay as you go
pay packet pay envelope
pay you out trick pay you back trick
pea-souper pea-soup fog
peckish starved
pedal bin step-on garbage can
pegs coat hooks, clothespins
pelmet valance *(for a window)*
pelting rain pouring rain
pence penny
pen driver pen pusher
Pension Scheme Pension Plan
peppercorn rent nominal rent
peppermint creams peppermint patties
Permanent Building Society Savings and Loan
  Company
personal call person-to-person call
personal experienced tuition, private tuition
  tutoring
physical jerks physical exercises
pick tooth toothpick
pickles *(pickled vegetables; (US) pickled cucumbers)*
pig's trotters pig's feet
pigs and whistles wrack and ruin
pike, to to speed
pillar box mail box
pinafore dress, pinny jumper
pinger oven timer
pips pits *(seeds in fruit)*

pitch field: I like an early morning game on the field at home.

Pity! Too bad!

pit orchestra *(section of a theater)*

plain as a pikestaff plain as the nose on your face

plate powder silver polish

playpark playground

play without stakes play for matches *(in a card game)*

plimsolls sneakers

plummy desirable

Point-to-Point Dance Hunt Ball *(for fox hunters)*

pokerwork woodburning *(work done by burning a design into wood with a heated metal point)*

polystyrene styrofoam

Pond Master *(man in charge of a swimming pool)*

ponging to high heaven smelling to high heaven

Pontefract cakes liquorice *(round liquorice candy originally made in Pontefract, Yorkshire)*

Poor beggar! Poor old sod! Poor wight! Poor blighter! Wretched fellow! Poor thing! Poor stiff! Poor devil! Poor slob!

porridge oatmeal

porridge stick wooden spoon

porter bock beer

post mail

pot hat bowler

pot head *(stupid person; (US) one who takes "pot," that is, marijuana)*

potato spirit *(alcohol made from potatoes)*

potholing spelunking

pots of money stacks of money

potty dotty, crazy: She was dotty about him.

power points electric outlets

powdered coffee instant coffee

power outage power failure

power socket electric socket

prang collision

prefect student monitor

prep homework

press studs snaps *(on clothing)*

price held price set, frozen

pricey, presy expensive

principal boy the lead *(in a play)*

Private Inquiry Agent Private Investigator, PI

private sitting bedroom roomette *(on a train)*

Privy Purse *(allowance for a sovereign's private expenses)*

Privy Seal *(seal used by or for the sovereign in subordinate matters)*

prize off pry off *(to remove a top from a container)*

prizeman scholarship winner *(winner of an academic prize)*

Prom *(abbreviation for Promenade, a concert during which the audience can move about; (US) a school or college dance)*

proprietary chapel *(a chapel that is private property)*

provision shop grocery store

pud pudding

pudding sleeve *(large, loose sleeve gathered at the wrist)*

pudding time dinner time

puff-puff choo-choo *(child's word for railroad train)*

pull a bit of a flanker to dope a horse

pull birds get chicks *(attract girls)*

Pull up your socks! Be sensible!

punters bookmakers

punting boating

push chair baby stroller

pushed for ready desperate for cash

put a term to it end it: He was having such a good time, it seemed a pity to end it.

put the mug on someone rub someone out *(to kill someone)*

put paid close the file on: We'll live to close the file on that mob of scoundrels.

Put up or climb down! Put up or shut up!

Put someone through. Put someone on. *(on a telephone)*

putting on side showing off

pyros firebugs

Quarter-wit half-wit

queen apple quince

Queer Street, being on being in dutch *(fictitious abode of persons in debt or having other difficulties)*

Queer Street booby hatch, insane asylum

queer bad money

queer *(odd looking, wierd (US) a person who favors his/her own sex)*

quick-change performer quick-change artist

quid, nicker, quidlet *(English pound)*

Quite absurd! Quite unsuitable! Terrible! Not right!

quizzing glass monocle

Race glasses binoculars

railway carriage, railway coach railroad car

railway engineers locomotive engineers

Railway Booking Hall Railroad Ticket Office

Railway Warrant Railroad Pass

railway railroad

rang called, phoned: Tell him I called.

ranker army private *(in a platoon)*

raree show side show

rare hard worker steady worker

rasher bacon slice

rat catcher *(unconventional fox hunting outfit)*

rate payers tax payers

Rating Authorities Tax Department *(of a community)*

Rattling good! Ripping! Smashing! Super duper! Great! Terrific!

raving gorgeous: I met a gorgeous Swedish chick.

read studied: I studied biochemistry at Harvard.
ready for off ready to go
ready reckoner adding machine
Reception Saloon Salon
recharge refill
Recorded Delivery Registered Mail
red rag tongue
red streak (*apple with streaked skin*)
Reduced to Clear Clearance Special
redundancy allowance severance pay
Redundant Shop Surplus Store
Refreshment Room Snack Bar (*at a railroad station*)
refuse van garbage truck
remarkably civil very nice: That's very nice of him.
resident homely woman housekeeper/homemaker
resident lady companion companion
retirement superannuation
return ticket round-trip ticket
returned elected
revenuers excisemen
revising reviewing: We've been reviewing that at school.
Ribena (*popular British black currant syrup which when diluted makes a refresing drink*)
ribstall gym bars (*wall bars used as exercise equipment*)
rick haystack
riding waistcoats riding jackets
rifle microphone shotgun microphone
Righto! Right-oh! Okay!
ring dial (*portable sundial*)
ring off hang up (*on a phone*)
road lamp street lamp
roadside pull-up diner
rock bun, rock cake raisin bun
roll-necked sweater, polo-necked sweater, pullover turtleneck sweater
rolling loaded: I've got an uncle who's loaded.
room-ridden roombound

rotovator rotary cultivator
rough and ready justice lynching
rough perfect almost perfect
rough-stuff (*coarse paint laid on after priming:* (*US*)*a fist fight*)
round fish (*any fish other than flat fish*)
round-headed puritanical
roundabouts merry-go-rounds
rout-cake (*a rich sweet cake for receptions, a "rout" being a large party*)
rowededow, rowdydow terrible din, hubbub
rowing boat rowboat
Royal Horse Guards, Blues (*the British Household's Cavalry Brigade*)
rubbish tip garbage dump
ruched-up frilled
rumbled caught on to, recognized
rumbo rum-punch
rum go a hard pull (*a difficult time*)
running up a score running into debt

S

Salad cream mayonnaise

Sale of Work Bazaar
saloon car (*car with an enclosed body*)
salt horse, salt junk salt beef (*sailor slang*)
sandwich tin cake pan
sanitary towel sanitary pad
Sanitation Department Department of Sanitation
sarky in a hurry, at a fast clip
scared blue, scared rigid scared to death
scatter-gun shotgun
scattered like billy be damned went like a shot
scent perfume
scheme plan
schmozzle, a a mess
school leavers, leaving students seniors, graduates
school speech-hall assembly hall

School Certificate, School Cert, School Leaving Certificates Diploma

scones biscuits

score off get the better of

scratch meal pot-luck

Scrutineer Poll Watcher

scud of wind gust of wind

screamer exclamation point

seasoning tub dough box *(trough in which dough is set to rise)*

see over look over: I'm hoping to look over the new house.

Self-Contained Set Private Suite

sellotape scotch tape, cellophane tape

send down expel *(from a school)*

senior to older than

Service Flat *(furnished apartment with linens, towels and a cleaning service)*

set one's face against something set one's mind against something

set up one's bristles raise one's hackles

shake down *(improvised bed; (US) forcing someone to pay you money)*

shark mannered rapacious

sharp as a needle sharp as a tack

sharp enough in a flash: If we'd lost, he'd have been over in a flash.

sharpset starved

sharp on-the-button

shaving tackle shaving gear

shift move off: They'll move off soon enough when they see us coming.

shilling *(10 pence)*

shingle pebble beach

shirty snippy, uppity: Stop being snippy with me.

shoot the moon take a powder, disappear: We must have good care that they don't take a powder.

shooter marksman

shooter rod, gun

shooting coat hunting jacket

shooting range rifle range
shop soiled shopworn
shop, to to sell down the river, to squeal on
shop walker floor walker
shopman storekeeper
shopping by post mail order shopping
Shopping Parade Shopping Center
shop store
short sighted near sighted
shot free scot free
shovel board shuffle board
sidebox *(box at the side of the theater)*
Sidesman *(deputy churchwarden)*
signature tune theme song
silk hat top hat
silver paper tissue paper
silverside top round steak
since the year dot since the year one
single bed twin bed
single cream light cream, half and half
single ticket one-way ticket
singlet undershirt, T-shirt
six of the best a caning, a hiding
skeletons in the cupboard skeletons in the closet
sketching block sketch pad
skipping rope jump rope
skirting board baseboard
slanging match *(a loud argument)*
slap-up dinner a special dinner *(with all the trimmings)*
slap-up stuff, catchpenny, brummagem junk
sleeping draught sleeping pill
sleeping suit pajamas
slide knot slip knot
sliding box drawer
slimming, banting dieting
slipover sleeveless sweater
slop-ins scuffs
slush counterfeit, bogus money

small fiddle, a a little bit of larceny

smalls, small clothes shorts, underwear

smarm smear, daub, plaster

Smartie-boots! Smartie-pants!

smock-frock smock

snide good stuff: You can't tell good stuff from bad.

snooker *(a variation of pool)*

snorkers sausages

soda scone soda cracker

solid as they come good as they come

somerset somersault

sort straighten out: I'll straighten her out soon enough.

sound as a bell sound as a dollar

soup squares bouillon cubes

sour lump of dough a difficult situation

soused herring marinated herring

souse pickled pig's feet or ears

speckless spanking clean

spinneys *(small clumps of trees)*

spit-box spittoon

spivvery black market operations

splash headings big headlines

spreading on the butter buttering someone up

spring onions scallions

spot of trouble a bit of trouble

sprat weather *(the dark days of November and December)*

square and aboveboard honest and aboveboard

squash *(fruit-flavored drink)*

Stalls Bar Refreshment Booth *(in a theater)*

stalls seats *(in a theater)*

stand for Parliament run for Congress

stand shot, stand treat to treat *(especially drinks)*

stand surety vouch: Will you vouch for him?

standard contract regular contract

stark raving crackers stark raving mad

starsheen starlight

starstone star sapphire

start fresh start over

starter appetizer

Stash it! Shush! Can it! Enough! Be quiet!

Station Master Station Manager

sticking plaster adhesive tape, band-aid

stickjaw *(sticky pudding or sticky candy)*

sticky wicket, a a difficult situation *(cricket expression)*

stir your stumps shake a leg: You'd better shake a leg and find her.

stirrup cup *(at a fox hunt, a cup of port or sherry taken on horseback, on arriving or departing)*

stock-jobber stockbroker

stocking ladders runs

stone cold cert a done thing

stony stone broke

storage jars canning jars, bell jars

store storage: The old-fashioned family pieces were taken from storage.

Stout fellow! Good guy!

stove-plant hot house plant

straightaway right away

straight play *(a play without music)*

strait waistcoat strait jacket

straw boater straw hat

streaky *(a type of bacon)*

street orderly scavenger

street furniture *(lamposts, parking meters, etc.)*

streety street wise

strongbox safety deposit box

Subpost Office post office branch

sugar basin sugar bowl

sultanas raisins

Summer Vac, Vac, The Hols, The Long, The Long Holiday summer vacation

summerset somersault

sums addition

supermarket trolley shopping cart

Supporting Programme Co-feature *(at a movie)*

Surgery Doctor's Office, Dentist's Office

surgical spirit alcohol

swan-shot buckshot
swedes rutabagas
sweep hand minute hand *(on a clock)*
sweet bay laurel
sweet oil olive oil, rape oil
sweet shop candy store
sweetie, sweety *(candy; (US) a loved person)*
sweeting *(a sweet apple)*
swing doors swinging doors
Swiss roll jelly roll
swoop surprise audit
swollen headed big headed
swot, a an eager beaver, a grind *(at a school)*
swotting it up, swotting cramming

T able water bottled water

Take a butcher's. Take a look.: Have you seen the
   evening papers? No? Then take a look at this.
Takeaway Take out *(signs on fast food stores)*
take eggs for money, to to make empty promises
taking it in good part being a good sport: I'm glad
   you're being a good sport.
takings net: There's a slight improvement in the net
   this month.
talk against time filibuster *(at Parliament)*
talk like a pen-gun talk like a machine gun
talk through the back of one's neck talk through
   one's hat
talkabout, a a talk show
tangas string bikinis
Tara! Tata! Ta! So long! See you!
Target Golf Range Driving Range
tattie bogle, bird scarer scarecrow
tatty ratty: She wore her ratty old raincoat again.
taxes rates
taxpayers ratepayers
tea-trolley tea-cart
teapot set tea set

tear off a strip give a severe scolding

teats nipples *(for baby bottles)*

teddy boys hoodlums

tedious codswallop stuff and nonsense: We're not standing for their stuff and nonsense.

telephone talkers obscene phone callers

telly TV

tenner *(ten pound note)*

termless endless

terraces row houses

Thank you very much indeed!, Thanks awfully! Thank you very much!, Thanks a lot!

That's a turn-up! That makes my day!

The best of British luck! Good luck to you!

The boot is on the other leg. The shoe is on the other foot.

The Exchange The Telephone Company

the Gold marigold

The Honorables, Hons *(daughters and sons of peers)*

The Household *(the royal domestic establishment)*

the May hawthorne tree

The line is engaged. The phone is busy.

The Offy liquor store *(short for "off license" meaning, their offerings must be consumed "off" their premises)*

The Smoke *(slang name for London)*

three-monthly quarterly

three times three *(three cheers repeated three times)*

thriller cliff-hanger

throw dust in one's eyes pull the wool over one's eyes

thundering good, awfully decent awfully good, very handsome: That's awfully good of you to do that for me!

tick and toy dilly-dally

tick off check off *(items on a list)*

tick one off tell one off

ticking over nicely moving along nicely

tidy bin waste basket

Time Bill Time Table

time for the joint dinnertime

tinned drinks cans of beer or soda

tinned meats canned meats

tin can

tin opener can opener

tipped cigarette filtered cigarette

to blot one's copybook to mess things up

to take a scunner on to dislike on sight

toe the bar toe the line

toffee, toffy taffy

togged up dressed up

toileted dressed

too much on one's plate overloaded, over one's head: I'm overloaded with things to do.

tooth glass toothbrush holder

top C high C

top-liner headliner

torch, electric torch flashlight

torpedo frankfurter roll, hot dog roll

touchlines sidelines: Cheering from the sidelines isn't much use.

towelling wrap terry robe

trade price cost price, at cost

trained nurse registered nurse

tram, tram-car trolley, street car

treacle molasses

tread upon eggs, to to walk on eggs *(being careful to not offend)*

trekkers hikers

trendy smart

trevira polyester

trilby, trilby hat fedora *(soft felt hat)*

trolley-man conductor

trolley gurney *(in a hospital)*

trump, a a doll *(indication of approval of what one has done)*: You're a doll!

trunk call toll call *(long distance telephone call)*

try it on the dog audience theater preview audience

try on, the the fitting *(of a dress or suit)*

tub frock washable dress

Tube, Underground, The Rattler Subway
tuck food *(eatables)*
Tuck in! Eat up!
tuck box *(food mailed by parents to school children)*
tuck shop *(pastry shop near a school)*
tumbled, twigged caught on
tuna steak, tunny tuna fish
turnups cuffs
twinset twin sweater set
two-fisted *(clumsy; (US) virile or vigorous)*

Ulster and topper raincoat and rainhat

underneaths underwear
undress shoes bedroom slippers, scuffs
Unknown Warrior Unknown Soldier
Union Jack Stars and Stripes *(flags)*
unwanted booking cancelled reservation
up a gum tree up the creek
up the spout down the drain
up to dick, up to the knocker up to snuff, up to par,
    up to declared value
up to one's eyes up to one's ears
up to time on time: Did he always turn up on time?
Up-Lines, Up Express *(trains going to city centers)*
**upping-stone, upping-stock, upping-block, horse
    block** *(block for getting up on a horse)*
urgency emergency: He's been called on an
    emergency.

Vacant tenancy vacant house, vacant apartment

valve radio tube
vegetable marrow zucchini, squash
visitor's stubs *(used at railroad stations)*
viva voce examinations oral exams

Wages car armored car

waist slip half slip

walk clerk (*one who goes around collecting proceeds of banks*)

walking out going steady

walking frame walker (*for an invalid*)

wallowing about in treacle being lovey-dovey

Warden Sexton (*of a church*)

wardrobe clothes closet

warning hooter alarm

was badly dipped lost a bundle

wash ball bar of soap

washhand basin bathroom basin, bathroom sink

washing bags laundry bags

washing line clothesline

washing-up dish washing

wasn't worth a day's purchase wasn't worth a dime

waste ground empty lot

water butt rain barrel

weak-minded simple minded

wear the breeches wear the pants

Welfare The Dole

Well met! Good to see you!

wellingtons, wellies rubber boots

wet canteen (*place on a military post where liquors are sold*)

wheeze, jape joke

white-bonnet shill (*at a fair*)

whip round pass the hat (*for contributions*)

who's-your-father what's-his-name: In this episode, he shoots what's-his-name.

wholemeal whole wheat

wide minded broad minded

wideawake hat (*low, wide-brimmed canvas or soft felt hat*)

wild carrot Queen Anne's lace

wild goose hunting wild goose chase

windcheaters windbreakers

window gazing window shopping

winkled sneaked: I sneaked myself in.

winkle pickers (*shoes with excessively pointed toes*)

will go to the wall will be history: The choir will be history if we don't help.

wipes, paper hankies kleenex, facial tissue

wit cracker wit

wizard super: We had a super lunch at the Lobster Pot.

won't wash won't work

wood-honey wild honey

wood-wool excelsior

woolies sweaters

work like a drayhorse work like a horse

work number business number

work to rule working according to the books

working like stink working like mad

Worthiest of Blood (*in a question of royal succession, a male as opposed to a female*)

wrap-around overall wrap-around apron

wrapover dress wraparound dress

wrapping papers gift wrap

wrong side of the stone walls wrong side of the tracks

Y ellow boy gold coin

yellow hammer finch

yellow weed goldenrod

yobbo (*tough hooligan*)

You've got it in one! You catch on fast!

Z ed zee (*the letter "Z"*)

zip fastener zipper, slide fastener

Zooks! Gadzooks! Goodness gracious!

AMERICAN-BRITISH
DICTIONARY

A to Z A to Zed

Accident Ward Casualty Ward

adding machine ready reckoner

addition sums

adhesive bandage, band-aid elastoplast, sticking plaster

affair do: I'm going to the charity do.

air gun air pistol

airplane luggage air case

aisle gangway *(in a theater)*

alphabet blocks alphabet bricks

alarm warning hooter *(on a plane)*

alcohol surgical spirit

All is not roses. All is not beer and skittles.

alligator bag crocodile-skin handbag

altitude zero altitude nil

aluminum foil leadfoil wrapping

ambulance blood-wagon

annual bus ride annual coach outing

apartment flat

appetizer starter

armored car bullion van, wages car

arson fire raising: Firemen were standing by should fire raising be reported.

As if I gave a hoot! As if I bloody well cared!

ashcanned *(cancelled):* The show was ashcanned.

as close as can be as near as dammit

asparagus grass, sparrow grass

assembly speech hall *(in a school)*

at a fast clip sarky *(in a big hurry)*

at cost at cost price

athletic event gymkhana

auto-race crash motor-racing smash

awful rush muck sweat

Back talk back-chat

back to the grindstone, back to the saltmines nose to grindstone

backpack haversack

bacon streaky: She bought milk and some streaky for breakfast.

bad manners bad form

bad mistakes crashing howlers (*in grammar*): You can correct the crashing howlers as they occur.

bad money, bogus money queer, slush

bad news Job's news

bad time, a a bad patch, a bloody awkward patch

Bad luck to them! Bad cess to them!

badger bullyrag

Baggage Check Cloakroom Ticket

Baggage Office Left-Luggage Office

bagging groceries parceling up groceries

baker's dozen devil's dozen, long dozen

Bakery Baker's Shop, Pastry Cook's Shop

baking chocolate cooking chocolate

bank account banking account

bank check banker's order

bank teller money pusher

Bank Clearing Houses Clearing Banks

Bankers Insurance Company City Guarantee Society

bar hop pub crawl

barber gent's hair dresser

bars pubs, the local, beer-offs

bartender barman, publican, barmaid

baseboard skirting board

bassonist faggotist

bathing suit bathing costume

bathroom bowl, bathroon sink bathroom basin, washhand basin

Bazaar Fancy Fair, Sale of Work

beat to the ground beat to sticks

be at one's best be on top of one's form

be damned be darned shot: What women see in him, I'll be darned shot if I know!

be high be in liquor

be homeless have the key of the street

be in a bind be in a bit of a cleft stick

be loaded have a long purse

be on pins and needles *(worried about an outcome)*

be saddled with be lumbered with

be treated badly be hard done by

beating a dead horse flogging a dead horse

bedroom slippers, scuffs undress shoes, carpet slippers

beets beet root

being a good sport taking it in good part: I'm glad you're taking it in good part.

being lovey-dovey wallowing about in treacle

being quiet lying doggo

being squeaky clean *(being in good standing, morally and professionally)*

belly wopping *(sleigh riding on one's belly)*

bicycle basket bicycle bin

bicycle headlight bicycle lamp

big mouth pan mouth

big shot big pot *(a show off)*

big talk rammel: All that rammel!

bikini panties minikinis

bill banknote *(paper money)*

Bingo Housey Housey

binoculars race glasses

birthday suit in the pink, starkers *(naked)*

biscuits scones

bit jot: There's not a jot of evidence for or against his story.

black as coal black as ink

blackberry preserves bramble jam

bloated bilious: I feel bilious.

blood-pudding black-pudding

blouse wooly

Blue Book *(a social register; (UK) a parliamentary publication with a blue cover)*

blueberries bilberries

boating punting

bobby pins hairgrips

bock beer porter

body-briefers cami-knickers

bone up, cram mugg up: You don't have to mugg up on that stuff.

boner clanger (*faux pas*)

booby hatch Queer street, laughing academy (*insane asylum*)

book mailing book-post

bookish booky

bookmakers punters

booth kiosk

boot licker, apple polisher lickspittle, pushful peeler

bored stiff bored rigid

born with a silver spoon in the mouth marked with a white stone

botch up clamper

bother nobble: Don't let them nobble you.

bottle pot: She bought a pot of nail varnish.

bottomless pit bottomless well: I'm not a bottomless well.

bought the farm, kicked the bucket went over the rainbow, dead as mutton, pegged out, pranged, went west, in the big dark, packed up, snuffed it, took the ferry, called it a day (*died*)

bouillon cubes soup squares

bouncer chucker-out

boutonniere buttonhole: Why aren't you wearing your buttonhole today?

bowler pot hat

box stall box (*at a theater*)

brainstorm brainwave

bran donkey food (*breakfast cereal*)

bread basket linen basket (*belly area of the body*)

bread board baker's board, moulding board

breakfast brekker

breaking point flashpoint: Every man has his flashpoint.

breaking the tape breasting the tape (*touching the finish line at the end of a race*)

breath mint kissing comfit

breath of air spot of air: They went out for a spot of air.

bright-eyed and bushy tailed (*happily alert*): She

always awakened bright-eyed and bushy tailed.

broad minded wide minded

broiler grill

Bronx cheer *(vulgar sound of disapproval made with the lips that originated in the Bronx, N.Y.)*

brown sugar demerara sugar

buckshot swan-shot

buck *(dollar)*

bullet holes bullet pocks

bulletin board notice board

bum around *(live dissolutely)*

bumbershoot brolly *(umbrella)*

bump on a log monkey-up-a-stick: Don't stand there like a monkey-up-a-stick!

bunch lot: Keep your eye on this lot.

bundle to choke a horse *(large amount of paper money)*

bundle packet: It'll cost you a packet.

burlap bags hessian sacking, crocus sacks

burp bring up the wind

buttering up someone spreading on the butter

bus driver busman

business number work number

busy signal engaged tone *(telephone)*

bus coach

Bye bye! So long! Ta! Cheery-o! Cheery bye! Bye!

BYOB party *(Bring Your Own Bottle party)*

C ad bounder

C.O.D., Cash On Delivery P.O.D., Pay On Delivery

cake pan sandwich tin

calfskin kipskin

called, phoned rung through

call shout: Shout when lunch is ready

camel hair coat camelcloth coat

campaign manager election agent

can of beer, soda tinned drink

can't make heads or tails of it can't make tops or bottoms of it

can't prove it by me. I know nothing about it.

can't take it can't stick it: I can't stick it anymore.

cancelled reservation unwanted booking

candy store sweet shop

candy sweets, gob-stoppers *(gob is slang for mouth;
   (US) gob is a U.S. Navy sailor)*

canned beverages tinned drinks

canned meats tinned meats

canning jars, bell jars storage jars

cap and gown full academicals

caraway-seed roll seedcake

carbonator gazogene, gasogene *(apparatus for
   making aerated water)*

cartoons joke drawings

case situation: We're working on a situation together.

cash lolly

casserole, one-dish meal fork supper

castanets, clappers knackers

cast lots draw cuts

catch up to someone catch someone up

cat's meow, the the cat's mustache

caught on, guessed tumbled, rumbled, twigged

chamois leathers

chancey dicey

charm mascot *(small pieces of jewelry for bracelets)*

chattering nattering, chuntering

cheaply on the cheap

check off tick off *(items on a list)*

Check room Luggage Room, Cloak Room *(A
   cloakroom can also be a rest room.)*

check bill *(in a restaurant)*

check checque *(at a bank)*

checkbook checquebook

checkers draughts

checking account current account

cheese cracker cheese biscuit

cheese cloth butter muslin

cheesy brummagem *(of poor quality)*

cherry soda cherry fizz

chewing gum fruit gum

chicken, yellow cowardly custard

chickpea Egyptian pea

chick bird *(slang name for "young woman")*

child abusers child bashers

chock full chock-a-block: For once the alley wasn't chock-a-block of cars.

choir organ chair organ

choked wuffed *(suppressed laughter)*

choo-choo puff-puff *(child's name for a railroad train)*

chopper eggbeater *(helicopter)*

chow down kip

cirrhosis of the liver whisky-liver

city gin adam's ale, adam's wine *(plain tap water)*

classic copybook: It was a copybook investigation.

classmate class fellow

clean as a pin clean as a new pin

cleaned valeted: I'll not go into that car until you have it thoroughly valeted.

Clearance Special Reduced To Clear *(sale signs)*

cloistered nuns enclosed order of nuns

close as can be, as as near as dammit

closed season close season, close time *(illegal hunting period)*

closet wardrobe *(for clothes)*

clothes hamper linen hamper, linen bin

clothesline washing line

clothespins clothes pegs

club sandwich *(double-decker sandwich)*

clumsy kack-handed

Co-Feature Supporting Programme *(at a movie)*

Co-op Market Co-op Foodhall

coaster cork drip-mat

coathooks pegs

cocktail lounge lounge bar

codfish ling *("ling" is also a name for "heather")*

coed *(female college student)*

coffee klatch coffee morning

coffin nails fags *(cigarettes)*

cold beer iced lager

cold frame cold house *(for plants)*

collection box collection bag *(in church)*

college entrance exams sit A-levels *(A-levels are "Advanced level" examinations.)*

colic, sulkiness mulligrubs

collar stay collar stiffener

come across with stump up with: I think you'd better stump up with the rent and taxes.

come around oil around: I expect Percy to oil around to my flat this afternoon.

Come out of the fog! Come out of the tall grass!

comedy routine comedy chat

comforter eiderdown

comic act comic turn: They're the best comic turn we've had here for years.

Commencement school leaving

commode close-stool *(portable toilet)*

Communion Rail Lord's Table

companion resident lady companion

complimentary ticket list free list: They were on the theatre free list.

concrete overcoat *(slang name for the concrete in which some criminals placed their enemies, after killing them, to weight their bodies when thrown into a body of water)*

conductor trolley-man

confectioner's sugar icing sugar

Congress adjourns Parliament rises

contribute pay in *(to a fund)*

converted stables mews *(flats)*

cook up something fox up something

cookbooks cookery books

cookie sweet biscuit

cookie box biscuit packet

cookies, crackers biscuits

cooperative forthcoming: I've been patient and forthcoming.

corn sugar dextrose made from maize

corncobs cobs of maize

cornstarch cornflour

corn maize *(All grains are called "corn" in the UK.)*

costly pricey

cot fold-up bed

cotton cotton wool

cough drops cough sweets, throat pastilles

counter clockwise anti-clockwise

County seat County town

cow-catcher *(apparatus on the front of a railroad*

train to throw off obstacles)

crabby cross-grained

cracker savoury biscuit

cramming swotting it up, swotting

crazy about frightfully keen on: She's frightfully keen on Victorian things.

crazy crackers: Don't listen to her, she's crackers.

credits credit titles *(acknowledgement of the work of participators other than actors projected on the screen at the showing of a film)*

crummy *(cheap or miserable; (UK) a cow with a crumpled horn)*

cubby hole dog kennel *(tiny cramped office space)*

cuffs turnups *(on trousers)*

cul-de-sac close

cup of tea dish of tea

cupcakes fairy cakes

curb kerb

Curtain time Curtain-up

custom-made bespoke, hand-cut

Cut it out! Knock it off! Beetle off! Stuff it! Push off!

cut rate stores cut price shops

cut throat cut-and-thrust: It was a cut-and-thrust business.

cutting ahead of cutting by *(another car)*

cutting costs cheeseparing

D.S.T., Daylight Savings Time B.S.T., British Summer Time

Damn it! Bugger it!

damned ruddy: They can do that a ruddy sight better than your **lot** (gang).

damned dumb bloody stupid: Don't be so bloody stupid!

damned foul up damn box-up: The whole thing was a damn box-up.

damned good thundering good: I had a thundering good time.

darned clever dashed clever

day bed French bed

day's work, a a hand's turn: He never did a hand's turn in his life.

deadbolts deadlatches

dead as a doornail dead as a herring, dead as mutton

delivery man roundsman

desirable plummy

desperate for money pushed for ready

detention jankers *(school or army punishment)*

dial tone dialling tone

diapers nappies

didn't have a penny to my name didn't have a ha'penny to rope together

dieting banting, slimming

difficult situation a sticky wicket *(cricket term)*

dig up *(acquire)*: What information did you dig up?

dig *(understand)*: I dig it.

dilly-dally tick and toy

dime *(10 cents)*

dimwitted bird-witted

dining tucking in: The French would all be tucking in economically at some sensible restaurant.

dinner bell dinner gong

diplomas school-leaving certificates, school certificates, school certs

dirty minded base minded

disappear in the night do a moonlight flit

dish it out *(give orders)* He sure can dish it out.

dish washing the washing up

diving board high board

diving gear diving kit

doctor's black bag doctor's tackle

Doctor's Office, Dentist's Office Surgery

doing nothing doing sweet all: I'm tired so I'm doing sweet all for a month.

doiley doyley

doing well being on form

doll, a a trump *(indication of approval of what one has done)*: You are a trump!

dollar, dollar bill *(100 cents)*

don't give a fig don't care a penny piece

Don't borrow trouble. Don't take your fences until you have to.

Don't get excited! Don't be getting your knickers in a twist!

Don't mess around! Don't muck about!

Don't mind him. You haven't to mind him.

done thing, a a stone-cold cert

Don't bite off more than you can chew! Don't bite off more than you can champ!

doo-dads fal-lals

Doomsday the last trump

dope a horse pull a bit of a flanker

double eagle *(gold coin worth $20)*

down the drain up the spout, down the loo

drainboard draining board

drawer sliding box

drawstring bag Dorothy bag

dressed to the teeth, dressed up like the cat's meow dressed up to the nines, smarmed up, in clobber, in ceremonial, dressed up like a dog's pillow

dressed up togged up, toileted

Dressing Room Retiring Room

dress frock

dried beans haricots

drinking buddy cupman

drivel crackling dottle

Driving Range Target Golf Range

dry goods store draper

drop a wrench in the works drop a spanner in the works

drug addict drug-taker: He's a confirmed drug taker.

druggist, drugstore chemist

drug nobble *(in reference to a horse):* They nobbled Top boy.

drumming one's fingers the devil's tattoo

dry as a bone, bone dry dry as a chip

dumb as they come simple as an egg

dumb bunny dumb brick

dumped all the answers in one's lap spilled secrets on one's plate

dumped dished: She was sure glad she'd dished him.

dust smut

E

Eager beaver, a grind a swot

ear muff earcap, earlap

Easter Parade Church Parade (*fashion parade after the church service*)

easy as pie easy as shelling peas

easy going jack easy (*to not care one way or the other*)

easy job cushy number

easy payment terms easy repayment schemes

eat away at nark at (*bother with persistent criticism*)

eat tuck in, tuck into

egg-plant aubergine, brinjal, brown jolly, mad apple, egg-apple, egg-fruit

elected returned

election time electiontide

electrical work electrics: I told my wife to get an electrician because I don't do electrics.

electric cord electric flex

electric outlets power points

emergency urgency: He's been called on an urgency.

emergency truck crash tender

empty lot waste ground

empty the cash register pinch the till: They rob small shops and pinch the till.

endless termless

engineer engine driver, train driver

English muffin muffin, crumpet

English ag: Put some ag on the ball.

English ivy ivy

enter into a contest with break a lance with

escape hatch funk-hole: It was a funk hole to be used for a quick getaway.

evaluation crit (*critique on the performance of a new teacher*)

even steven (*equal numbers on each side*): We'll go even steven on the booty.

Everythings hunky-dory! All's well!

Everythings jake. Everything's fine.

exactly spot-on: My version came out at 17 syllables spot-on.

excellent, A plus full marks

excelsior wood wool

exclamation point screamer

Exit Way Out

expel send down *(from a school):* He was sent down from Oxford.

expensive pricey

expensive gift pricey presy

expensive gown posh frock

Express Letter Special Delivery

Extreme Unction Last Unction *(last rites of the Catholic church)*

eye cup, eyewash eye bath

Fair Fete

fake stuff slap-up stuff

faking shamming round

false alarms hoax calls

family car family saloon

fantastic bloody marvelous

fast freight express goods

fast set the rapid set

Fat chance! Dog's chance! Not an earthly!

fed up to the teeth fed up to the back teeth

fedora trilby, trilby hat, billycock *(soft felt hat dented lengthwise)*

feel wierd suddenly come over queer

feeling a bit off the weather feeling a bit dicky

feeling flush feeling chuft: I was feeling quite chuft.

feeling hungry feeling a bit peckish

feeling ok feeling fit

field pitch: I like an early morning game on the pitch at home.

fifth wheel, a a gooseberry

filet mignon fillet steak

filibuster talk against time

filtered cigarette tipped cigarette

final grades pass-out marks

financial meeting costing meeting

financial wizards financial boffins

finish off, close the file on, end it put paid

finished the course passed out: He passed out.

fire bugs pyros

fire drill kerb drill

fired, let go cashiered, sacked, got one's cards, got the books, got to the wall, got the bucket

first car leading coach *(of a train)*

first floor *(the ground floor; (UK) the floor above the ground floor)*

first place tie joint first

fish croquette fish cake

fish sticks fish fingers

fish store fishmongers

fish truck fishmonger's van

fit as a fiddle fit as a flea

fitted rubber boots half-wellingtons

fitting, the the try-on

flag waving flag wagging

flagstone walk crazy paving

flag standard

flare up, a a blaze-up

flashlight torch, electric torch

flesh brush back scrubber

flight before last the last flight but'one

flim-flam a bit of bunch

floor walker shop walker

flounder plaice *(a fish)*

fly-fisherman fly-fisher

fog lights fog lamps

Foggy Bottom Jaw Factory on the Thames *(slang names for Washington, D.C. and for Parliament)*

Food and Drug Administration, FDA Committee on Safety of Medicines

fooling around slap and tickle: All that kissing and slap and tickle.

foolproof plan foolproof wheeze

fool gammon

football player footballer

footprints footmarks

Forget it. Don't mention it. Not at all.

Fork it over! Give it to me!

formica laminate
found by chance chance-found
found out caught out: I could get caught out.
foxglove dead men's bells
foxy dishy (*glamourous*)
frankfurter, hot dog hot dog sausage sandwich
frankfurter roll, hot dog roll torpedo
freak shows freak-peeps (*at a fair*)
free installation free fitting
free of charge cost-free, free cost
french fries chips
fresh milk new milk
fried eggs with onions eggs in moonshine
friendly the matey kind
frilled ruched-up
from now on in future
fruit peddler's truck costermonger's cart
full remittance (*full payment*)
full steam ahead full belt: He went full belt.
funny as can be rowdy-dowdy
fuss argy-bargy

Game leg gamey leg
gangbuster gang-breaker
garbage can dustbin
garbage dump rubbish tip
garden hose hosepipe
garden party garden fete, lawn party, lawner
gauge bore: He hunts with a 12 gauge shotgun.
gave it up chucked it
gear kit
gelatin jelly
German silver British plate
get a word in edgewise get a word in edgeways
get along get on
get back on one's feet find one's feet
get mugged get set on
get nervous get the pip
get one's dander up get or have one's monkey up
get the better of score off

get the wrong end of the stick get the dirty end of the stick

get to know chat up

get under one's skin get under one's wool

Get going! Get moving! Get cracking! Get weaving!

getting along getting on: How are you getting on?

gets beet red assumes a prawn-like hue

gig *(musician's club date)*

gingersnap gingerbread biscuit

girl's bicycle ladies cycle

give a good try have a go: I've been having a go at it.

give a hand bear a hand: Can you bear a hand with this chair.

give one the heave-ho, give one the boot give one the toe of one's boot

give one's eyes for something give one's ears for something *(wanting something badly)*

give one what for *(a severe scolding):* I told my son's teacher that if he played hooky again, I would give him what for!

give up throw in

gladiolas corn flags

glasses giglamps *(spectacles)*

go bananas go bonkers

go downhill *(deteriorating health)*

go even steven *(to divide evenly)*

go for broke, go whole hog neck or nothing

go-getter goer

go haywire go poopsie

go off half-cocked go off at half cock

go on the lam do a bunk

go over with a bang go over with a swing

go up the river *(go to jail)*

Go ahead! Carry on!

going full steam ahead going full belt

going like crazy going like Billy-O *(swift as William, the Conqueror's invasion of Britain)*

going steady walking out

going under going up the spout *(a failing business)*

golf cart golf trolley

good as they come solid as they come

good fellow, good guy decent sort, stout fellow

good stuff snide: You can't tell the bad stuff from snide.

Good Book Bible

Good luck to you! The best of British luck!

Good Night Sweetheart God Save the Queen (*the last number played at a dance or ball*)

Good to see you! Well met!

Good work! Wonderful! Good! Well done! Ripping! Smashing! Super! Goodoh! Jolly good show! Capital! Blimey!

goof, a a boob

gorgeous raving: I met a raving Swedish dish (girl).

gosh-awful: You've always had the most gosh-awful nerve.

got it down pat got it pat

grab bag: I'll buy your ticket and bag some seats.

graduated fully qualified

graduates, seniors leaving students, school leavers

graduation party diploma-do

graham crackers digestive biscuits

grain corn (*To the British, any kind of grain is "corn." Our corn is called "maize."*)

grand, a (*$1000*)

granulated sugar caster sugar

grapevine, the the bush telegraph (*slang for gossip*)

grasp at straws snatch at straws

grass clippings grass mowings

grateful for small favors grateful for small mercy

grave the long home

great player, a a bobby dazzler (*in soccer*)

Great speech! Well said!

green thumb green fingers

Grievance Day Paper Day

Grin and bear it! Grit your teeth and soldier on!

gripe, a a grumble

grits (*crushed maize*)

grocery chain multiple grocer's

grocery store provision shop

ground meat minced meat

Guidance Counselor Careers Master

gum drops fruit pastilles

gun shooter

gurney trolley *(at a hospital)*
gust of wind scud of wind
gym bars ribstall
gym suits games tunics

H
ad it copped a basinful: Your brother looks as if he's copped a basinful.
hair clip hair slide
hairpin turn hairpin bend
half dollar *(50 cents)*
half slip waist slip
half-wit quarter-wit
halter woman's backless *(type of dress)*
hamburger buns country baps *(country baps are smaller but similar and used as rolls)*
ham gammon
hand cuffs darbies
hand puppet glove puppet
hang up ring off *(end a telephone conversation)*
Hang on. Hold on *(telephone expression)*
hard candy, jawbreaker hard sweet
hardware store ironmonger
hash browns *(shredded and fried potatoes)*
hate their guts hate their entrails
have a bad time of it have the black ox tread on one's foot
have a bee in one's bonnet have a bee in one's trousers
have a boarding house reach make a long arm *(to help oneself freely at the table)*
have a frog in the throat *(being hoarse)*
have plenty on hand keep a good house *(food)*
have pull *(having influence to get special favors)*
Have a seat! Take a pew! Have a chair!
have have done: She upset her daughter more than she need have done.
having a ball having some laughs, enjoying it frightfully
having a grandfather of a fight having a mother and father of a row

having a lot of nerve cheek: I have a lot of cheek coming to you about this.

hawthorne tree The May

hay fever hay asthma

haymakers *(powerful punches with a fist; (UK) "Haymakers," a country dance)*

haystack rick

hazel nuts, filberts Kentish cobs

He's a dilly! He's a daisy!

head liner top-liner

headlines, big splash headings

head nurse matron

head-shrinker *(psychiatrist)*

heads or tails cross and pile *(game)*

healthy fit

hearing aid deaf-aid

heartfelt homefelt

heat lamp health lamp

heavy cold heavy chill

heavy cream double cream

hedging hedge buying *(at a Stock Exchange)*

heeled *(wealthy; (UK) having a gun)*

Hey! I say!

high C top C

high price a long figure

hikers trekkers

hit the nail on the head was spot on: At the meeting, Old Twining was spot on.

hitchhike catch a lift

hitting the sack kipping down

hobby-horse bobby-horse *(merry-go-round horse)*

hocus-pocus jiggery-pokery

hodgepodge hotchpotch

homefree home and dry: We thought you were home and dry.

homely *(someone who is not pretty or handsome; (UK) pertaining to the home, familiar)*

homework prep

honest and aboveboard square and aboveboard

honey hive honey

hoodlums teddy boys

hoofer *(dancer in a chorus line)*

hook a ride cadge a lift

hootch, hooch whiskey

hop about on crutches halt on two sticks

horse block, upping-stone, upping-stock, upping-block (*aid for getting on a horse*)

horseback riding horse riding

horse vaulting horse (*wooden horse used for gymnastic exercises*)

hot house plant stove plant

hot line hush line

Hot diggety dog! I'm over the moon!

housekeeper/homemaker resident homely woman (*see "homely"*)

housekeeping home-keeping

How awful! How ghastly!

How do you like your coffee? Are you black or white? (*meaning, "Black or with milk?"*)

hungry peckish

hunt ball point-to-point dance (*ball for fox hunters*)

hunting jacket shooting coat

hush puppies (*fried balls of corn meal*)

I get the point. I take your point.

I have a bone to pick with you. I have a crow to pick with you.

I must be going. I must be toddling along.

I should live so long. No way! Not on your life! Like fun! Like boggery! Not half! Not for nuts!

I'll buy that. (*agreement*)

I'll clue you in. (*relating all the latest information*)

I'll eat my hat if it isn't so. I'll eat my boots if it isn't so.

I'm indebted to you. I'm no end obliged.

I'm off and running! (*meaning: "I must hurry!"*)

I'm very sorry. I'm extremely sorry.

ice bucket ice pail

ice cream cone ice-cream cornet

ice cream sandwich slide

ideal husband pattern husband

identification bracelet identity bracelet

if push comes to shove... *(meaning: "If a confrontation is inevitable, then...")*

If the shoe fits. If the cap fits.

in a bind in a bit of a cleft stick

in a flash sharp enough: If we'd lost, he'd have been over sharp enough.

in a hurry in a muck sweat

in a jiffy in a brace of shakes

in a sec, in a minute in a tick

in chronological order in date order

in due time in the fullness of time

in dutch on Queer street *(having money troubles or other difficulties)*

in good shape, in the pink in fighting fit, in the pink of health

in no time in a canter

in so many words in terms

in the altogether naked

in the doghouse in chancery *(in disgrace)*

in trouble in bother, in the cart

in two shakes of a duck's tail, in two shakes in two shakes of a duck's whisker, in two ticks flat, in two twos

Income Tax Inland Revenue Duty

income the comings-in

innocent as a newborn babe innocent as a babe unborn

instant coffee powdered coffee

instructions the drill

insurance plan insurance scheme

Intermission Interval

Internal Revenue Service, IRS Inland Revenue

investors investment firm subscribers

Irish soda bread soda bread

It hit me! The penny dropped!

It sure was awful. It was a sour lump of dough.

It won't work! It's a fizzle! It won't wash! It's a swizz!

It's a date. It's fixed.

It's a hard pull. It's a rum go. *(resolving a difficulty)*

It's great! It's wizard!

It's in the bag. It's a cert!
It's so beautiful! It's dashed beautiful!
It's the real McCoy. It's the real McKay.

Jelly doughnut jam doughnut

jelly roll jam roll, Swiss roll
jimmy jemmy *(burglar's short crowbar)*
joke jape, wheeze
JP, Justice of the Peace C.P., Clerk of the Peace
jumper pinafore dress
jump rope skipping rope
jumpy sarky *(impatient)*
junk bumf, Brummagem, catchpenny
just the same all the same

Kangaroo court *(unauthorized court which
   disregards the principals of law and justice)*
**keep something on the quiet, keep things under
   one's hat** keep one's thumb on
keep track of keep oneself informed
Keep track of the time. Mind the time.
Keep your trap shut! Hold your jaw!
keeping one's eyes peeled keeping one's eyes skinned
kerchief head hugger
key holder key fob
kidney bean, butter bean French-bean
kid cheek: He loves to cheek his parents
killer a croaker
kissy kissy matey
kite flying kiting
kleenex wipes, paper hankies
knapsack haversack
knickers knickerbockers
knock up *(to make pregnant; (UK) to rouse someone
   by knocking)*
knocked for a loop knocked sideways: She had a
   smile that knocked him sideways.
knuckle sandwich bunch of fives *(the clenched fist)*

Ladyfingers sponge fingers

lamppost lamp standard

large majority thumping majority: He won by a thumping majority.

latex paint emulsion

laugh, joke giggle, jape: We did it for a giggle.

laundry bags washing bags

lazy louts layabouts

lead principal boy *(in a play)*

left holding the bag left holding the baby, standing shot

lemon drop acid drop

lemon soda, lemonade lemon squash

let one down do one down

Let's give it another try. Let's have at it again.

Let's go for broke! Bugger the consequences!

Let's have a talk. I'd like a word with you.

Let's take it as it comes. Let's take it by numbers.

letter size foolscap size

lewd behavior chambering

light cream, half and half single cream

light fixtures light fittings

light pole lamp standard

like a house on fire like houses on fire

like a kick in the teeth like a kick in the head

like a ton of bricks like a sack of coal

like being in a goldfish bowl like living in a shop window

like clockwork like a clock

like falling off a log *(easy):* Sure I can do it. It will be like falling off a log.

likes fancies: He fancies you.

lily-livered cowardly

line queue

linoleum lino

linsey-wolsey winceyettes

liquor store The Off-License, The Offy

little bit of larceny a small fiddle

loaded, well-heeled rolling, having a long purse: I've got an uncle who's rolling.

locker room changing room

London fog London pea-souper
Lonely Hearts Club Love Monger
long distance calls trunk calls
long johns *(long underwear)*
look, a a dekko: Let's have a dekko at her.
look over see over: I'm hoping to see over the new house.
looking like a million, looking great looking like a thousand pounds, looking like 30 shillings in the pound
looks lit up like Time Square looks like the Blackpool illuminations
looped bottled, foxed, screwed, tiddly, squiffed, potted, whiskified
lost a bundle was badly dipped
Lost and Found Lost Property Office, Left-Luggage Office
lowboy trailers low loaders
lowest rates keenest rates
luggage carts luggage trolleys
lump of butter knob of butter
Lunch Room Dining Hall *(in a school)*
lynching rough and ready justice

Machine washable dress tub frock

macs, macintoshes *(apple variety; (UK) raincoats)*
made a boo-boo dropped a clanger, made a bloomer
made quite a stir caused quite a flutter in the pigeon loft
magnifying glass burning glass
mail order shopping shopping by post
mail truck postal van
Mail Box Letter Box, Pillar Box
mail the post
Main Street High Street
make a date fix a time
make a fuss kick up a dust
make a great start go off at score
make an appointment fix a day
make-up cape toilet cover, toilet cloth
making some good money making a good penny

man's bicycle gent's cycle

marksman shooter

match lucifer

mayonnaise salad cream

mean *(person who hurts others in word or deed; (UK) stingy)*

Meat head! Meat-brain! *(name calling)*

meat turnover pasty

Medical Society Medical Council

Medicare National Health Insurance, N.H.I.

Men & Women's Rest Rooms Men & Women's Open Toilets

merry-go-rounds roundabouts

mess, a a schmozzle

messed things up blotted the copybook, made a bloody hash of it, made ducks and drakes of things

messy job the slogging bit

messy scatty: All that scatty hair flying around.

mid-term half-term

migraine megrim

mile a minute nineteen to the dozen: They were chattering nineteen to the dozen.

milk delivery truck milk float

milk run *(pilot's routine flight; (UK) milkman's morning round)*

minute hand sweep hand *(on a clock)*

miserable weather beastly weather, filthy weather

miserable flipping, blooming: It's a flipping waste of energy.

Miss Prim Miss Prunes and Prisms

mistress, prostitute fancy woman

molasses treacle

monocle quizzing glass

moolah, bread, folding green, ready cash, simoleons, mazuma lolly, shekels, the ready, dibs, oof *(slang for money)*

more than you can shake a stick at *(a great number)*

mortar board college cap

move off shift: They'll shift soon enough when they see us coming.

movies cinema, the films, the pictures

moving along ticking over: The research projects were ticking over nicely.

moving man van man

moving van, furniture truck pantechnicon, pantechnicon van, removal van

Much ado about nothing! Great cry and little wool!

Music Director, Conductor Chapel Master (*in a church*)

Nail polish nail varnish

near sighted short sighted

neat jemmy, gemmy

necklace necklet

nervy (*bold; (GB) nervous or excited*)

net takings: There's a slight improvement in the takings.

nickel (*5 cents*)

Night School Night Class

nightgown nightdress, bedgown

nip and tuck rum go: It's rum go and no fooling.

nipple teat (*on a baby bottle*)

no good, a a bad lot: He's always been a bad lot.

no great shakes (*not very good*): As an actor he's no great shakes.

No swearing aloud! No ruddy swearing aloud!

nodding acquaintance chatting acquaintance

nominal rent peppercorn rent

nonsense kerfuffle: You always take a lot of kerfuffle from him.

Nosiree bob! Not a chance in a million! Not a hope!

not as good as not a patch on: His new job is not a patch on the job he lost.

not for love or money not for luck or love

not one's business not one's pigeon

not to know your nose from your elbow not to know "B" from Battledore

not up one's alley not up one's street

not with a ten foot pole not by a long chalkmark, not by a long chalk

Notary Public Commissioner for Oaths

nothing worth taking nothing worth nicking

nothing, zip nil: We lost 100 to nil.

Now you're talking big money. Now you're talking in imperial measures.

nuts, crazy daft, crackers: You're daft!

nutty as all get out daft as they come

Oat cracker oat cake

oatmeal porridge

obscene phone callers telephone talkers

odd jobs man hobjobber, casual

odd rum: He's a rum sort.

off the rack clothes off the peg clothes

Okay! Righto! Right-oh!

Old Glory, The Stars and Stripes The Union Jack (*affectionate names for the American flag and the British flag*)

Old pal Dear boy, Old mate, Old fruit

older than senior to

olive oil sweet oil

on a pin-head on a three-penny bit: You could write all you know about marriage on a three-penny bit.

on credit, on the cuff on tick: I'll try to get it on tick.

on equal footing on terms

on-the-button sharp

on the first try on the first go: You can't expect perfection on the first go.

on the fritz (*not working*): This socket is on the fritz.

on the go on the trot

on the sidewalk on the pavement

on the up and up, legit genuine

on time up to time (*punctual*)

one-way ticket single ticket

Operating Room Operating Theatre

oral exams viva voce examinations

orchestra the pit (*a theater section*)

ordinary people suet puddings: The Swanns have been suet puddings for generations.

ordinary too normal by half

out of breath blown, puffed out

out of business in the cart

out of date overdated
out on the town on the razzle
outfit oneself kit oneself
oven mitt oven glove
oven timer pinger
over head and heels over head and ears
overcoat greatcoat
Overdraft *(delinquent notice from a bank)*
overreaching overshooting
overtired, worn out, exhausted, beat, all done in
  overspent, knackered, whacked

P ackage packet, parcel

pajamas pyjamas, sleeping suit
pale ale bitter beer
pampered high fed
pantry larder
pantyhose tights, pantytights
paper towels kitchen paper
paraffin *(wax for candles or coating: (UK)*
  kerosene)
parenthesis brackets
Parent's Day Open Day *(parent's visiting day at a*
  school)
parka anorak
pass the hat whip round: She'll whip round this
  afternoon.
patent leather japanned leather
path footway
patsy *(naive person)*
pawn shop leaving-shop
pay as you go pay as you earn
Payment on Delivery Carriage Forward
peanut monkey nut
peapod peacod, peascod
peas pease
pebble beach shingle
peddle flog: He was off to flog the stuff he'd been
  stealing.
pencil pusher pen driver
peeved narked
penny, cent pence, "p", penny-piece

Penny Arcades Fun Arcades

Pension Plan Pension Scheme

peppermint patties peppermint creams

peppers capsicum

percentage of the take lolly *(illicit money)*

performer turn: The great Eugene had been a very popular turn.

perfume scent

period full stop

periwinkle pin-patch, pennywinkle *(edible snail)*

person-to-person call personal call

phone booth, telephone booth call-box, telephone-box

phys. ed. instructor games mistress, games master

physical exercises physical jerks

pick up tidy up

pickles *(pickled cucumbers; (UK) pickled vegetables)*

pie crust dough paste

pie flan

pig's feet pig's trotters

pile of loot lump of brass *(money)*

pimp fancy man

pits pips *(grapefruit or orange seeds)*

plain as the nose on your face plain as a pikestaff

plane kite

plan scheme

play fifth wheel play gooseberry

play the innocent come the innocent

played for a sucker *(deceived):* I don't like being played for a sucker.

playing stupid games playing silly-ass

playground play park

pleased as punch cock-a-hoop: You should be cock-a-hoop over that.

points marks *(used for scoring in sports)*

poison tipple *(slang for drink):* What's your tipple?

polish something off *(finished):* He polished off his meal in minutes.

polyester trevira

poor manners bad form

Poor thing! Poor devil! Poor stiff! Poor beggar! Poor sod! Wreched fellow! Poor blighter!

popsicle iced lolly
portable baby bed Moses basket
post office branch subpost office
Post Office The Post
pot-luck scratch meal
potato chips crisps
pouring rain pelting rain
powdered eggs egg-powder
power failure power cut
practically a baby straight out of the egg (naive): It's just that you are straight out of the egg.
pregnant in pod
Prepaid Delivery Carriage-Paid
preview audience try it on the dog audience
price frozen, price set price held
primer absey book *(ABC book)*
principal of a school headmaster, headmistress
private ranker *(in an army platoon)*
Private School Public School *("voluntary schools," meaning: parents pay tuition for their children)*
proctor invigilator
provide tea lay on tea
prowlers night intruders
prune French plum
pry off prize off
public relations man constituency agent
public transportation public transport
Public Ballroom Assembly-Room
Public School Council School
pull the rug out *(leave one without resources)*
pull the wool over one's eyes throw dust in one's eyes
pullover jumper
pumps court shoes
punch line the cruncher
punch someone's face clean someone's clock
puritanical round headed
purloin cabbage
put on the spot *(in danger or in an untenable position)*
put someone on put someone through *(on a telephone)*
put the bite on *(ask for money)*

put the kibosh on put paid *(ended):* This has put paid your little game.

putting on the dog putting on side

Put up or shut up! Put up or climb down!

Quarterly three-monthly

quarter *(25 cents)*

Queen Anne's lace wild carrot

questioned blackguarded

quick-change artist quick-change performer

quince queen apple

quotation marks inverted commas

Racket row: There was a motorcycle making a row at the front door.

radio set

railing at fate kicking at the bricks

railroad car railway coach, railway carriage

railroaded *(swift action without careful consideration):* He railroaded the motion through the committee.

Railroad Ticket Office Railway Booking Hall

Railroad Railway, Gridiron, Teakettle

rain barrel water butt

raincoat and rainhat ulster and topper

raincoats mackintoshes, macs, macks, waterproofs

raining like crazy, raining cats and dogs raining like Billy-O

raise one's hackles set up one's bristles

raisin bun rock bun, Bath bun

raisin cookie Garibaldi

raisins sultanas

rapacious, is has shark manners

rat hole cat-hole *(a tiny office)*

Ready-Get-Set-Go! Ready-Steady-Go *(said at the start of a race)*

real mess, a, a darn shame a jolly shambles, a mug's business

real well jolly well: You've done jolly well so far.

Real Estate Tax House-Tax, House-Duty

realtor estate agent

really sorry genuinely sorry

record player gramophone

recording secretary minutes secretary

red letter day (*very important day*)

redhanded, in the act on the hop: He caught them on the hop.

refill recharge: He urged her to recharge her glass.

Reform School Juvenile Hall

Refreshment Booth Stalls Bar (*in a theater*)

registered nurse trained nurse

Registered Mail Recorded Delivery

regular attendance keep a term (*at school*)

regular contract standard contract

Regular Mail Ordinary Letter Post

rental hire charge

reservation list booking board

reserve fix: I'll fix a court at the club.

Retirement Superannuation

Revenuers Excisemen

reviewing revising: We've been revising that at school.

revivalist preacher hot-gospeller

rib, kid jape: Who are you trying to jape?

rib roast chine of beef

rich posh

riding jackets riding waistcoats, hacking jackets

rifle range shooting range

right as rain, right as can be right as a trivet, right as ninepence

right away straightaway

right on the money, right on target, right on the nose bang on

robe dressing gown, morning gown

rocks, ice (*diamonds*)

rod shooter

roombound, shut-in room-ridden

roomette private sitting bedroom (*on a train*)

roommate chamber fellow (*at a boarding school*)

rotgut cheap whiskey

rotten like dust (*contemptible*)

rough-stuff *(a fist fight; (UK) coarse paint laid on after priming)*

round-trip ticket return ticket

row for pull for

row houses terraces

rowboat rowing boat

rubber boots india-rubber boots, wellies

rubber neckers kerb-watchers

rubber cement cow gum

rubbers overshoes of india rubber, gumboots

ruckus kickup: All that kickup about expenses.

ruffled, fluted smocks gaufer-stitched smocks

rumble seat dickey, rumble-tumble

Rummage Sale Jumble Sale

run for Congress stand for Parliament

run for office be a candidate

run up a debt run up a score

running ticking over: The engine was ticking over sweet and true.

rush beetle

rutabagas swedes

rye bread, wholewheat bread brown bread

Saddled lumbered: We don't want to be lumbered with him if we don't have to.

safe as can be safe as houses

Safety Deposit Box Strongbox

salary heist wages raid

salon reception saloon

salt away money *(save money)*

salt beef salt horse, salt junk

sanitary pad sanitary towel

Sanitation Department Sanitary Authorities

sausage and mashed potatoes sausage and mash

sausages bangers, snorkers, faggots

Savings and Loan Bank Building Society

scads of money pots of money

scarecrow tattie-bogle, bird scarer

scared stiff scared rigid

scholarship winner exhibitioner, prizeman

school vacation break up, shut down, the hols

school transcript curriculum vitae

School Taxes Education Rates

scoop is, the the buzz is *(meaning: reliable information has it that...)*

scotch tape, cellophane tape sellotape

scot free shot free

seats stalls *(in a theater)*

second hand clothes store duddery

seconds export rejects

secret marriage hedge marriage

sell down the river shop: I never thought I'd shop George.

selling drugs dealing drugs

sell, to flog

set one's mind against something set one's face against something

setting the table laying table

sewing kit sewing outfit, housewife

sexton warden

shadowing sentry-go

shake down *(to extort money from someone; (UK) an improvised bed)*

Shake a leg! Stir your stumps!

sharp as a tack sharp as a needle, brisk as a bee, keen as mustard

shaving gear shaving tackle

shill nobbler

shirr pucker *(make gathers in materials)*

shoe button eyes boot-button eyes

Shoe Store Boot Shop

shoelace, shoestring bootlace

shoot off one's mouth *(tell all one knows)*

shooting the breeze *(chatting)*

shoo chivvy: He began to chivvy the dogs out of the room.

shopping bag holdall

shopping cart supermarket trolley

Shopping Center Shopping Parade

shopworn shop soiled

short bread short crust

short evening jacket bum-freezer

short term short dated

shotgun microphone rifle microphone

shotgun scatter-gun

should have should have done: Conservation didn't appeal to him. Perhaps it should have done.

shoulders to the wheel backs to the wheel

showing off putting on side

showy materials fancy goods

shrimp cocktails prawn cocktails

shuffle board shovel board

Shush! Stash it!

sick as a dog dog sick

side effects back-kick

side road side turning

sidelines touchline: Cheering from the touchline isn't much use.

sideshow raree show

sideways edgeways: It's difficult to get a word in edgeways.

simple minded weak-minded

since the year one since the year dot

skeletons in the closet skeletons in the cupboard

sketch pad sketching block

skinny dipping *(swimming nude)*

skip it, pass it by give it a miss

slaved beavered away: He beavered away polishing all my brass.

sleeper *(movie that becomes very popular with little advance publicity)*

sleeping pill, sleeping powder sleeping draught

Sleeping Car, Sleeper Cross-Sill

sleeveless sweater slipover

slide fastener, zipper zip fastener

slingshot catapult

slip knot slide knot

slot machine fruit machine

small roll bap *(resembles a hamburger bun)*

smart trendy *(usually in reference to fashion)*

smart alecs clever dicks

smarter than one looks cleverer than one looks

Smartie-pants! Smartie-boots!

smelling to high heaven ponging to high heaven

smidgeon *(very small amount)*

smock overall, smock frock, smicket

smooth as silk *(very smooth)*

snack spot of dinner: We'll have a spot of dinner and go on from there.

snaps press studs *(on clothing)*

snapshot, shot snap *(a photograph)*

sneakers plimsolls

snow goggles snow spectacles

So who cares! So stone the crows!

soap, bar of washball

sorehead *(angry person):* Don't mind him. He's a sorehead.

soccer football

soda cracker soda scone

somersault summerset

sound as a dollar sound as a bell

sound effects noises-off: There were plenty of noises off in this movie.

soundless keyboard dumb piano

spanking clean speckless

spareribs bones

spatula palette knife

special dinner slap-up dinner *(with all the trimmings)*

spelunking potholing

spike-heeled shoes spindle-heeled shoes

spittoon spit-box

spoken for bespoken: I'm bespoken.

spool of thread cotton reel

sprinkles hundreds-and-thousands *(tiny colored candies used to sprinkle on cakes and cookies)*

spuds mash *(potatoes)*

squash, zucchini corgettes, vegetable marrow, marrow

squealed, tattle-tailed grassed

stacking trays build-up trays *(in an office)*

stacks of money lots of brass

stain on one's reputation a hole in one's coat

stand firm stand to: Has she enough pluck to stand to?

staples general stores

star attraction, starring role star turn

star sapphire starstone

stark raving mad stark raving crackers

starlight starsheen

starved sharpset, peckish, ravening

station wagon estate car, shooting brake

step-on garbage can pedal bin

stick one's nose into things stick one's long ears in things

sticks out like a sore thumb *(is very evident):* His discontent sticks out like a sore thumb.

stickup *(robbery; (UK) a stand-up collar on a shirt)*

stockbroker stock-jobber

stockinet elastic knitted textile fabric

stocking runs stocking ladders

stone broke stony

store bought out of a packet

storekeeper shopman

stores shops

storm windows double glazing

stove cooker

straight arm, to to ward off

straight down evendown: The rain came evendown.

straight jacket strait waistcoat

straight pins household pins

straight razor cut-throat razor

straw hat straw boater

street lamp road lamp

street wise streety

stretching the truth drawing the long bow

strike breaker, scab black leg

string along hoax, josh

string bikinis tangas

string tie bootlace tie, narrow tie

stringing it out *(taking a long time to get to the point)*

stroller push chair *(for a baby)*

Student Monitor Prefect

studied read: I read biochemistry at Cambridge.

studio apartment bed sitter, combined room

Stuff and nonsense! Tedious codswallop!

stuffed with bunged up with: We're just bunged up with starchy foods.

stuffy stivy

styrofoam polystyrene

Subsidized Housing Council Houses

substituting doing a locum *(taking the place of a doctor or minister)*

Subway Tube, Underground, The Rattler

such a dope mardy *(dense)*

sugar bowl sugar basin

sulphur and molasses brimstone and treacle

Super! Super duper! Super-do! Wizard! Rattling good! Absolutely top hole!

suspenders braces

swan dive fancy dive

sweaters woolies, jumpers

sweetie *(a loved person; (UK) candy)*

swimming pool, pool swimming bath, baths

swim bathe

swinging doors swing doors

T -shirt, undershirt singlet

tack pin

taffy toffee, toffy

tailor whipcat

take a dislike to take a scunner on.

take a fall *(fall down or fail in business)*

take a nap have a lie down

take empty promises take eggs for money

Take Out Takeaway *(fast food signs)*

take someone on take someone up *(to cultivate someone)*

Take a look at this. Take a squint at this. Cast your eye over this. Take a butchers. Run your eye over this.

talk like a machine gun talk like a pen-gun

talk show a talk about

talk through one's hat talk through the back of one's neck, to the backbone through and through

talk turkey *(talk bluntly)*

talking a blue streak *(talking rapidly)*

talking one's ear off chatting up: He's chatting up some girl at the bar.

tanked-up (*drunk*)

tattle-taleing tale-bearing

Tax Department Rating Authorities

tax collectors excisemen

taxes rates

taxpayers ratepayers

Ticket Office Booking Office

tea-cart tea-trolley

tea cloth (*towel used to wash the tea things*)

tea party muffin fight, muffin worry, bun fight

tea set teapot set

tea tray tea board

teddy, teddy briefer camiknicker

teetotaler a TT

Telephone Book Directory Inquiries

telephone exchange line

tell one off tick one off

teller, bank clerk counter clerk

tempest in a teapot storm in a teacup

ten-gallon hat (*cowboy's broad-brimmed hat*)

terrible din, hubbub rowededow, rowdydow

Terrible! Quite absurd! Bloody awful! Quite unsuitable!

terribly bright frightfully brilliant

terry robe, terrycloth robe towelling wrap, bath wrap

TGIF (Thank God It's Friday) (*favorite Friday expression in the U.S*)

thank you letter a roofer (*for hospitality*)

Thank you just the same. Thank you all the same.

Thank you so much. Thank you very much. Thank you ever so. Thank you very much indeed.

Thanks a lot. Thanks awfully.

That did it! That does it! That's torn it! That's put the tin lid on it!

That makes no never mind! (*doesn't matter*)

That's a tall order! That's a bit much! That's a bit sweeping.

That's a good fellow! That's a good chap!

That's another story. That's another pair of shoes.

That's awfully good of you. That's awfully decent of you.

That's great! That's rich! That's champion!

That's highway robbery! (*the price is exorbitant*)

That's not in my ball park. (*not one's area of expertise*)

That's old news! Oh, Queen Anne's dead!

That's one for the books! (*a very surprising event*)

That's that! That's settled then!

the four hundred, the upper crust the upper ten (*the top four hundred in American society, the richest, (UK) the most prominent*)

the jig's up up goes the monkey

the john the bog, the loo

the low-down the gen (*actual facts or inside information*)

the messy situation they're in the dog's dinner on their plates: We'll be far away before they straighten out the dog's dinner on their plates.

the stage the boards

the winner at the head of the poll (*in an election*)

The cat is out of the bag! The fat is in the fire!

the cat's meow the cat's mustache

The phone is busy. The line is engaged.

The Polls The Polling Station

The shoe is on the other foot. The boot is on the other leg.

The Telephone company The Exchange

theater aisles gangways

theme song signature tune

thickets coverts

think back to cast your mind back to

through thick and thin in weal and woe

throw a monkey wrench into the works throw a spanner in the works

throw in the sponge throw up the sponge

throw up chuck up

thumb tacks drawing pins

thumbing his nose cocking a snoot

ticket stub counterfoil

Tic-Tac-Toe Naughts and Crosses

tied in first place joint first

Time Table Time Bill

to be short to be in low water (*having little money*)

to be treated badly to be hard done by

to begin with for a start

to hit against a snag strike a bad patch: I've struck a
bad patch and hope you can help me.

to mess things up to blot one's copybook

to my fingertips to the boot soles: I'm a peasant to the
bootsoles.

toe the line toe the bar *(to follow the rules)*

togs gear *(clothes)*

toll call trunk call *(long distance telephone call)*

too smart for her own good too clever by half

Too bad! Tough going! Pity! Worse luck! Hard
cheese! Hard graft! Hard luck!

toothpick pick tooth

top hat chimney pot hat, silk hat

top round steak silverside

tossing off knocking back: He was knocking back a
lot of champagne.

tote bag Dorothy bag

tough as leather tough as old boots

toughs hard boys

tour bus tourist bus, charabanc

townspeople townees

traffic jam traffic block

train gate barrier *(at a railway station)*

trap shooting clay pigeon shooting

treat stand shot, stand treat

tricks dodges

trolley, street car tram, tram-car

truck cab driving cabin

tube valve *(for a radio)*

tunafish tuna steak

turned out ok turned up trumps: His son has turned
up trumps after all.

turtleneck sweater roll-necked sweater, roll-neck
pullover, polo neck sweater

tutoring personal experienced tuition, private tuition

tutor coach

twin bed fold-up bed

twin sweater set twinset

two-fisted *(virile, vigorous; (UK) clumsy)*

two-nothing two-nil *(game scoring)*

Unlisted ex-directory *(on the telephone)*

U. S. Congress Parliament

U.S. Bonds National Savings Certificates

Uncle Sam Old Blighty *(affectionate names for the US and Britain)*

underwear smalls, underneaths

under the weather *(feeling ill)*

Unemployment Office Labour Exchange

Universal Suffrage Household Franchise, Household Suffrage

up-chuck up-throw, up jack

up in the air getting the breeze up: You're getting the breeze up about nothing.

up the creek up a gum tree

up to par, up to snuff up to the knocker, up to standard, up to dick

uppity shirty: Stop being shirty with me.

Vacant house or **apartment** vacant tenancy

vacuum cleaner hoover

valance pelmet *(for a window)*

very nice remarkably civil: That's remarkably civil of him.

very religious churchy

vest waistcoat, gilet

Veterans Hospital Disabled Soldiers Institute

voters constituents

voting district constituency

vouch stand surety

Wake up calls alarm calls *(at a hotel)*

walk on eggs tread upon eggs

walk over walk round: I'll walk round to see you.

walker walking frame

wallet, billfold notecase, notebook, ladies purse notecase, man's notecase

wall-to-wall rug fitted carpet

Ward Common Ward *(of a hospital)*

washable dress tub frock

wasn't worth a dime wasn't worth a day's purchase

waste basket tidy bin

Watch out! Panic stations!: Panic stations, the boss is looking for you.

Watch Your Head Mind Your Head

water paint colour washing

waving a hankie flipping a wiper

weak as a kitten weak as water

weaken flag: Try not to flag.

wear the pants wear the breeches

wearing one's best bib and tucker (*wearing one's best clothes*)

weather stripping draught excluder

week ago Monday last Monday week

weekly offering church rate

Welfare The Dole

went like a shot scattered like billy-be-damned

wet behind the ears no oil on one's feathers

wet blanket, party pooper dry file

wetsuit frogman suit

what's-his-name who's-your-father: Get who's-your-father in here.

wheat bread corn

wheel chair wheeled chair, Bath chair, invalid chair

while back, a backalong: I worked with her backalong.

white raisins sultanas

white sneakers mutton dummies

whole shebang, the whole enchilada the whole bloody lot

whole wheat whole meal

wholesale firm cost-sale house

wild honey wood-honey

wildcat strike lightning strike

will be history will go to the wall: The choir will go to the wall if we don't help.

win first place bear the bell, carry off the bell

windbreaker windcheater

window shopping window gazing

wine storeroom buttery

win make a broadside

won't do a darn bit of good won't do a blind bit of good

wooden spoon porridge stick

working according to the book work to rule

working like mad working like stink, going at it hammer and tongs

worn out fagged, knackered

wrack and ruin pigs and whistles

wrap-around apron wrap-around overall

wraparound dress wrapover dress

wreckers breakers

writer ink slinger

wrong side of the tracks wrong side of the stone walls

You catch on fast! You've got it in one!

You slay me! *(You are very amusing.)*

Zero, zilch nil

zipper, slide fastener zip fastener

zip nip: I nipped up the road at a fast clip but she was out of sight.

> "The time has come," the Walrus said,
> "To talk of many things
> Of shoes-and ships-and sealing wax-
> Of cabbages-and kings..."
>
> *Through the Looking-glass*
> *Lewis Carroll*

PHRASEBOOK

TRAVEL ESSENTIALS

Accommodation

Tourist Boards regularly inspect the thousands of places to stay in Britain and they are classified according to the range of facilities and services provided. Those having higher quality standards will have **Approved** (**Merit** in Wales), **Commended, Highly Commended** or **Deluxe** next to the Crown designation; the maximum designation being **Five Crown.**

Note: Be sure that the price quoted is "all found" (all inclusive) so there won't be any extras on the final bill.

ACCOMMODATION WORDS

alarm call — wake-up call
bath — bathtub
bed-sitter or **combined room** — studio apartment
block of flats — apartment house
clothes pegs — clothes pins
desk porter — desk clerk
digs — furnished apartments or houses
dustbin — garbage can
face flannel — face cloth
flat — apartment
flex — electric cord or wire
fitted carpet — wall-to-wall rug
fold-up bed — cot

French bed — daybed
geyser — gas water heater
hoover — vacuum cleaner
immersion heater — electric water heater
lifts — elevators
lodger — renter
power points — electrical outlets
public convenience — restroom
self-contained set — private suite
semi-detached house — duplex
service flat — furnished apartment with linens,
    towels and cleaning service
single bed — twin bed
tidy bin — waste basket
washing line — clothes line

Currency

In 1971, England adopted **"decimalization"** and the **£** (pound sterling) was divided into 100 pence, known generally as **"p"** (pronounced "pee"). Coins are 1p, 2p, 5p, 10p, 20p, 50p and £1. All are round in shape except for the 20p (small in size) and 50p (large), which are seven-sided and silver in color. Paper bills are £1 (Scotland and the Channel Islands only) £5, £10, £20, and £50. A price is usually given as "One-fifty" meaning "One pound, fifty pence" Anything below a pound, is said as "80p" or "80 pence." You will get more pounds for your dollars at banks and money exchanges. The official rate of exchange is listed at both, as well as at airports and hotels. You can get cash at automatic teller machines if your home bank is connected with a UK bank. Banks are open Mondays to Fridays from 9:30 to 3:30 and some may also be open Saturdays from 9:30 to noon.

Note: The British Tourist Authority advises that credit cards are not widely accepted in Britain, especially at B & B's (Bed and Breakfasts) and that retailers have the option to charge more for purchases and services obtained by a credit card.

MONEY AND BANKING WORDS

at short sight — payable on presentation
banker's order — bank check
bank notes — bills (like dollar bills)
checques — checks
counter clerk — teller
current account — checking account
delinquent notice — overdraft
feeling chuft — feeling flush
fiver — five pounds
keenest rates — lowest rates
note-case — wallet
on tick, on the slate — on the cuff
pots of money — stacks of money
quid, nicker, quidlet — one pound
stand surety — vouch for
strong box — safety deposit box
three monthly — quarterly
to run up a score — to run up a debt
stoney, skint — stone broke
tenner — ten pound note

Chunnel

One can now cross over to France in 35 minutes from Folkestone, West Sussex, to Calais, France, 24 hours a day, every day of the year, by Channel Tunnel, popularly known as the **"Chunnel."** The Chunnel was officially inaugurated on June 6, 1994 by Queen Elizabeth II and French President Francois Mitterrand.

The trains run at speeds of up to 187 mph at depths from 80 to 150 feet below the sea bed. They provide three types of service: **Cargo,** which carries trucks on double-decked train cars; **Le Shuttle,** a car-, bus- and motorcycle-ferry service which runs every 15 minutes, each train carrying up to 80 automobiles; and **Eurostar,** train service for **"foot traffic,"** that is, travelers without a vehicle which takes only 3 hours between London's Waterloo station and Paris' Gare du Nord. It has 794 seats and provides meals for first class passengers. Second class can buy snacks.

Disabled, Facilities for:
Free information and advice on suitable hotels and other facilities is available from the Holiday Care Service, 2 Old Bank Chambers, Station Road, Horley, Surrey RH6 9HW, England. Ask the British Travel Authority for a Holiday Care Service enquiry form.

Driving in the UK

DRIVING TIPS

1. Safety Hint: While driving, repeating to oneself: **"I must stay on the left side of the road."** can be a great help, especially when rounding a corner. It will help to suppress that overpowering urge to swing to the right side of the road.
Note: Seat belts are mandatory for front-and-back-seat passengers.

2. Driver's License: A **US Driver's License** or an **International Driving Permit** allows one to drive in Britain for up to 12 months. Most rental companies require that you must have had your license for at least a year.

3. Car Rentals: Cars can be rented at any **hire car firm** (rental car company). A car with an **automatic steerer** (automatic transmission) is easier to drive for anyone unused to driving on the left-hand side of the road. Most rental companies require that the **rental charge** (passenger liability, third party, fire and theft insurance) be paid in advance. Ask for instructions on how to use the **emergency telephone boxes**.
Note: In case of an accident, dial 999 to summon help and 122 to summon police.

4. Car Repair Should your car break down, a **breakdown van** (tow truck) will take your car to a **breakdown service garage** (auto repair shop) . There,

panel beating will remove dents, **burst tyre punctures** will be mended and the engine checked.

CAR PARTS

back mirror — rear mirror
bonnet — hood
boot — trunk
bottom gear — low gear
car locker, glove box — glove compartment
demister — defroster
driving mirror — rear view mirror
engage gears — shift gears
exhaust silencer — muffler
faschia board — dash board
filler cap — gas tank cap
gear lever — gear shift
half shaft — rear axle
handbrake — parking brake
headlamp — headlight
mileometer — odometer
number plate — license plate
roof lamp — dome light
shoulder belt — shoulder harness
shockers — shocks
spanner — wrench
sparking plugs — spark plugs
trafficators, indicator lights — turn signals
tyres — tires
windscreen — windshield
windscreen wipers — windshield wipers

5. **Petrol (Gasoline):** Petrol is graded by one to four stars. **Four star petrol** would be equivalent to American high-test gasoline. It is leaded and 97 octane. **Unleaded petrol** comes in two grades: **Premium 95 octane** and **Super 98 octane.** Petrol is sold by the **imperial gallon**, 4.55 litres (liters) or 1.2 gallons. *Note: Many petrol stations are closed on Sundays so be sure to get your gas tank filled ahead of time.*

ROAD SIGNS

Bypass — Detour
Car-Park — Parking Lot
Careful-Loose Chippings — Careful Fresh Gravel
Clearway — No Parking Along Highway
Double Bend — S-Curve
Flyover — Overpass
Give Way — Yield
Hairpin Turn — Hairpin Bend
High Road — Highway, Main Road
High Street — Main Street
Keep To the Near Side Except For Passing —
 Keep to the Left Side Except For Passing
Lay-By Verges — Roadside Parking
Level Crossing — RR Crossing
Metaled Road — Macadamized Road
No Entry — Do Not Enter
No Overtaking — No Passing Zone
No Through Road — Dead End
Outlooks — Overlooks
Overbridge — Railroad Bridge
Pavement or **Footway** — Sidewalk
Pull-ups — Diners
Roadworks — Construction Zone
Roundabout — Traffic Circle, Rotary
Side Turning — Side Road
Sliproad — Ramp
T-junction — Road Ends At a T
Traffic Signal — Traffic Light
Trunk Road — Main Road
Unmade Road — Dirt Road
Verge, Grass Verge — Road Shoulder

Electricity

The standard voltage throughout the UK is 240 volts
AC, 50 HZ cycles. A three square-pronged adapter,
and/or converter is necessary unless you have a dual
voltage device. A plug adapter set is necessary to deal
with different plug configurations.

Health

The British Travel Authority strongly advises that one take out adequate insurance coverage before traveling to Britain because the only treatment that is free is emergency treatment requiring out-patient treatment at National Health Service Accident and Emergency Departments of hospitals. Check this out with your insurance company and travel agent. If you're **feeling poorly** (feeling too sick), to see a National Health Service doctor, ask a telephone operator for the nearest **Surgery** (Doctor's Office). For light ailments, a **dispensing chemist** (pharmacist) will be able to help. Should you need prescription drugs, you should have with you a copy of your prescription plus a cover letter from your doctor. Drugs should be described by their generic names in case American brands are not available; also, it may be necessary that the drugs be prescribed by a British doctor before a chemist will fill the prescription. There is a fee for the dispensation of medicines on prescription. Chemists have window signs saying they have a dispensary inside. Some stores which only sell toiletries and related goods are called Chemists or Drugstores to distinguish themselves from Pharmacies. **"BOOTS"** is a chain of "chemist's shops."

Note: For emergencies, dial 999 and ask for "Ambulance." If you can get there yourself, go to the nearest hospital Casualty Department (Emergency).

HEALTH WORDS

back kick — side effects
bilious — bloated
bring up the wind — burp
cast one's waters — urinalysis
casualty — accident
come over queer — feeling weird suddenly
cottonwool — cotton

cough sweets, throat pastilles — cough drops
chuck up — throw up
knackered, fagged — worn out
Matron — Head Nurse
overspent — overtired
Sister — Nurse (whether male or female)
trolley — gurney

Post Office

Post Offices are open from 9:30 to 5:30, Monday-Friday and from 9:00 to 12:30, Saturdays. Stamps are also sold at Postal Centre stamp dispensers in large stores and major tourist attractions. News-agents who sell postcards may also have stamps.

POST WORDS (MAIL WORDS)

express — special delivery
G.P.O. — General Post Office
letter box, pillar box — mail box
ordinary letter post — regular mail
packet — package
recorded delivery — registered mail
shopping by post — mail order shopping

Telephone

April 16, 1995, the British telephone system inaugurated two major changes: first, all dialing codes would now have a 1 after the initial 0, for example, **0171 instead of 071**; and second, all international dialing codes from the UK changed from **010 to 00**. British Telecom and Mercury Communications provide the telephones in Britain. The push-button public phones accept coins of any denomination and there are also Phonecard payphones which accept pre-paid Phonecards. British Telecom Phonecards can be obtained from post offices and shops displaying the green Phonecard sign. Mercury phones are operated by your own credit cards or by special Mercury telephone cards obtainable from newsagents and nearby shops.

Important U.K. phone numbers:
999: emergency assistance
192: local and countrywide information
100: local operator
155: international information and operator

Note: To save expensive hotel telephone charges when calling home, use the services of AT&T, MCI and SPRINT. The numbers to use should be on your credit cards.

TELEPHONE WORDS

be on the telephone — listed in the directory
call collect — reverse the charges
dialling tone — dial tone
Directory Enquiries — Telephone Book
engaged tone — busy signal
exchange line — telephone line
Give me a ring. — Call me.
Hold on! — Hang on!
hush line — hot line
Internal Telephone — in-house phone at a hotel
not on the telephone — unlisted in the directory
personal call — person-to-person call
Put (someone) through — Put (someone) on
rang off — hung up
rang through — called, phoned
Telephone Kiosk, Telephone Box, Call-Box —
   Phone Booth
telephone talkers — obscene phone callers
The Exchange — The Telephone Company
The line is engaged. — The line is busy.
trunk call — toll call, long distance
Trunks — Long Distance Operator
work number — business number

Time

In Britain, as in all of Europe, the 24-hour clock is used on all official documents and timetables but not in general conversation. *To use it, subtract 12 from any number greater than twelve.* The UK also observes Daylight Savings Time but calls it **British Summer Time (B.S.T.)**.

The Old Royal Observatory, built by Sir Christopher Wren in 1678, is the building where "time began." **The world's measures begin here** with the prime meridian, 0 degrees longitude running through the building. **Greenwich Mean Time** is the standard by which every clock in the world is set. The Observatory is now a museum with 600,000 visitors a year. Greenwich can be reached in 20 minutes by BritRail from London's "London Bridge" Station.

TIME WORDS

ack emma and pip emma — A.M. and P.M.
alarm calls — wake-up calls
anti-clockwise — counter-clockwise
backalong — a while back
between the lights, between two lights, the half dark — twilight
five and twenty past — twenty-five after
fixed up — made a date
fixture — appointment
fortnight — two weeks
for donkey's years — for ages
Half a mo! — Half a sec!
in a tick — in a sec
in date order — in chronological order
in two two's — in two secs
Mind the time! — Keep track of the time!
overdated — out of date
sharp-on-the-button — exactly on time
since the year dot — since the year one
summer-tide — summer time
sweep hand — minute hand

Tipping

Hotels: A 10 to 15% service charge is usually added to the bill so no tip is required. Should there be no service charge, then 1£ a day should be adequate.

Restaurants: Some include a service charge. If no charge is added, then 10 to 15%.

Porterage (Porter service): 50 to 75p per suitcase.

Taxis: 10 to 15% of the fare *Generally one waits in a queue for a taxi.*

Hairdressers: 10 to 15%; and 50p to the assistant who washes your hair

Trains

If the train is one's travel choice, it's advisable to **book** (reserve) a seat well in advance even if you have a BritRail Pass. It's most essential for sleeping car arrangements. There are eight main train terminals in central London, each dealing with a specific region. Check ahead for the one needed. Tickets are purchased at a **Railway Booking Hall** (Railroad Ticket Office). Most long distance trains have both **standard** (tourist class) and first class carriages and one can choose a **coupe'** (a half compartment) or a **cross-sill** (full compartment for sleeping accommodations). First class tickets cost about 50% more than standard class and usually include a restaurant and/or buffet car. Restaurant cars have two sittings. Ask the train steward for a mealtime card. Available are: **single tickets** (one-way tickets), **return tickets** (round-trip tickets) or cheap **day returns** (going and coming the same day). Tickets should be held as the ticket collecter will take them on the train or at the **barrier** (train gate) when one leaves the train. **Luggage trolleys** (luggage carts) are available for **cases** (suitcases). Baggage can be checked at the **Left Luggage Office** (Baggage Room). Lost property is held at the **Lost Property Office** (Lost and Found). Railway stations have **Conveniences** (Rest Rooms) and **Refreshment Rooms** (Snack Bars).

MORE TRAIN WORDS

Check Room — Baggage Room
cloakroom ticket — baggage check
engine driver, train driver, railway engineer —
   railroad engineer
goods train — freight train
halt, a — a train stop
leading coach — first car
private sitting bedroom — roomette
railway carriage — railroad car
railway warrant — railroad pass
retarded — delayed
Time Bill — Time Table
Up-Express — towards London

VAT (Value Added Tax)
There is a national VAT charged on all hotel, restaurant
and **car hire** (rental car) bills and as these are
considered services, this VAT cannot be refunded. The
VAT can be refunded on purchases made in **shops**
(stores) affiliated with **Europe Tax-Free Shopping
(ETFS).** Look for the **"Tax-Free for Tourists"** logo
in their windows. Show your passport and ask the clerk
for a **"tax free shopping voucher."** Keep all your
purchases in a separate bag and on leaving the UK, take
the goods and voucher to the Customs desk to be
stamped and cash it , minus a handling fee of about
20%, at the **ETFS Booths** at London Heathrow,
London Gatwick, Manchester, Glasgow and Stansted
Airports.

Weather
British weather is noted for changing suddenly so a
raincoat, folding umbrella, and clothing that can be
layered for warmth would be a wise precaution. The
following is the average daily temperature, as furnished
by the British Meteorological Office, based on 1966-90
averages.

	Jan	Feb	Mar	Apr	May	June
°C	4	4	6	8	11	14
°F	39	39	42	46	52	57

	Jul	Aug	Sept	Oct	Nov	Dec
°C	16	16	14	11	7	5
°F	60	60	57	51	44	41

Examples of how one converts Celsius to Fahrenheit and vice versa:

$$C \quad 30°C \times 9/5 = 270/5, = 54, +32 = 86°F$$
$$F \quad 86°F - 32 = 54, \times 5/9 = 270/9, = 30°C$$

WEATHER WORDS

beastly, filthy weather — miserable weather
**lashing down rain, raining like Billy-O, pelting
   rain** — pouring down rain, raining cats and dogs
pea-souper — London fog
scud of wind — gust of wind
sprat weather — dark days of November and
   December
punishing rain — unending rain

LONDON

London, as Home Base
London is usually the first stop for visitors and it has such a drawing power that many opt to locate there with occasional day trips elsewhere. Besides the usual sights: the Tower, the Changing of the Guard, etc., there is another very popular visiting site courtesy of Queen Elizabeth...a tour of part of Buckingham Palace's 540 rooms. Other sights worth visiting are the long buried Anglo-Saxon Sutton Hoo Treasure at the British Museum, The Bank of England, the homes of Dickens and Dr. Johnson, William the Conqueror's Domesday

Book at the Public Record Office, the Botanic Gardens at Kew and the leafy neighborhoods of Hampstead and Richmond.

London, Transportation:
Taxis: London's **hackney carriages** (taxis), the **famous black cabs**, have very courteous and informed drivers whose characters have been checked out by Scotland Yard. They have to earn their licenses by two years of training involving knowing all the 750 miles of London's streets.
Subway: The world's oldest subway (100 in 1963) and the longest in miles of track is called the **Tube,** the **Rattler** or the **Underground.** It was the haven for many Londoners during the bombings of WWII. Its major routes are colored red, blue and green.
Buses: City buses are red. You pay the conductor on his rounds and hold onto the ticket until you leave. **Tour buses are green** and travel 40 miles outside of London. There are day trips and half-day trips to many famous places such as: Windsor Castle, Hampton Court, Oxford, Brighton, Bath and Stratford-Upon-Avon, Shakespeare country.

THE PEOPLE

Architecture and Archaeology
In viewing the beautiful buildings, churches, Roman ruins and stone and iron age artifacts in Britain, your guides may be using unfamiliar architectural and archeological words and terms. A glance down the following list may be helpful:
Bailey — fortified courtyard of a castle
Barbican — tower used to defend the entrance to a castle
Baroque — means "irregularly shaped"; an Italian style popular in 17th century Europe
Barrow or **Tumulus** — burial mound
Cairn — a pile of stones atop a prehistoric grave
Caryatid — a column with female figure

Classical — styled after Greek and Roman buildings

Curtain Wall — the outer wall of a castle

Donjon or **Keep** — the strong central tower to which a garrison retreated when hard pressed

Elizabethan — the Renaissance-Gothic mixture that succeeded Gothic

Folly — a structure built for decoration with no architectural purpose

Gallery-graves — oblong underground graves

Georgian — (1714-1810) period of the four Georges

Gothic has three periods: *Early English* with pointed arch (end 12 century); *Decorated* with elaborate decorations (early 14 century); and *Perpendicular* with vertical window tracery, vaulting and panelled walls (late 14th to mid-16 century)

Gothic Revival — late 18 and 19 centuries

Ha-Ha — a sunken ditch edging to a garden

Jacobean — period of James I of England (1603-25), a mixture of Gothic and Classical

Lady Chapel — usually placed behind the high altar and dedicated to the Virgin Mary

Megaliths — large blocks of stone

Menhirs — ancient large standing stones

Neo-classical — mid-18 century revival of the Classical style

Palladian — symmetrical and pedimented style introduced to England by the Italian, Andrea Palladio (1518-80)

Passage Graves — circular mounds of earth or stone that are entered by a long, narrow passageway

Portcullis — a strong castle gate that can be raised and lowered

Rood-screen — an ornamental screen separating the Chancel from the Nave of a church

Tessellated — Roman mosaics made up of tiny pieces of stone, tile or marble embedded in cement

Tudor — period of the Tudor regents, 1485-1603; brick was the material most used.

Victorian — 1837 to 1901, mostly Gothic Revival and Greek Revival architecture

Wattle-and-daub — interlaced flexible twigs plastered with a mixture of clay, chopped straw and horsehair which early man used for walls and fences

Crime and Police

Note: This section and that of the Law is dedicated to the lovers of British mysteries.

THE POLICE: The Police patrol their beats without guns, handcuffs or gas canisters. They only carry concealed wooden **truncheons** (clubs). They consider their job to be keeping the peace. They can carry arms during dangerous assignments but must return them when the assignment ends. They still try to follow the concept of Sir Robert Peel, the Home Secretary in 1829, that the police were not a military force, rather, a civilian body mixing with a civilian population. He prescribed a non-military uniform that was practical and dignified with a special helmet which took his name, the "bobby" helmet, and his police were called **"bobbies"** and **"peelers."**

POLICE TOOLS, STATIONS, WORK AND PRISONS

Black Maria — police van
bluebottles, busies, coppers, pigs, rozzers, slop, fuzz — slang names for the police
dabs — fingerprints
darbies, gyves — handcuffs
fingers, grasser, nose, spiv, copper's nark, snout, rattler — stool pigeon
gaol, jug, quod — jail
on dab — on report
on remand — in custody awaiting trial
on the roster — on duty
out on license — on parole
Pixie — police minibus
police burgh — police district
police outrider — police escort
put a watch on — a stake-out

The Dock — court

The Yard — Scotland Yard, now called **New Scotland Yard** since it moved from its original headquarters located on the site of a medieval palace which housed Scottish royalty on their visits to London.

upperstocks — ankle restrainers

warder — jailer

CRIME WORDS

backhand or **dash** — a bribe

bent — crooked

bit of bunch — a flim-flam

bumbaze — bamboozle

burke — stifle, kill

cabbage, crib, nick, snaffle — steal

charley, to — to act sneakily

claret — blood

converted — embezzled

cooked the books — doctored the books

cosh — blunt instrument

crack a crib — make a break-in

cushy number — pushover

cut one's stick, do a bunk, hop the twig, cut one's luck, hook it, scarper — to cut out, leave, hide

dibs and dibstones — money and jewels

dicey — chancey

dodges — tricks

fire raising — arson

foolproof wheeze — foolproof plan

funk hole — escape hatch

gang-breaker — gangbuster

have someone on, sell smoke, nobble — to swindle

heeled — having a gun

hoax calls — false alarms

jemmy — burglar's jimmy (crowbar)

lolly — illicit money

long firm — fake company

nasty piece of work — predator

nip a bung, cut a purse — purse snatching
pinch the boodle — steal the swag
pipe off — case a joint
pocket pickers, dips — pickpockets
popped — pawned
put a cheat upon — deceive
rumbled — caught on to
shove the queer — pass bad money or slush
snatchers — shoplifters
to shop, to blow the gaff — to sell down the river
winkled — sneaked

CRIMINALS

chummy — small time crook
child bashers — child abusers
con merchants, confidence tricksters —confidence
men
crack rope — one deserving to be hanged
cut purse, nipper, dip, pocket picker — pickpocket
hard face — soulless, relentless criminal
hedge creeper, jack hasty — sneak
night intruders — prowlers
shifty looking basket — a sneaky pete
smasher — one who passes bad money
snatcher — shoplifter
spring heeled jack — one who makes a quick
getaway
**teddy boys, yobbos, pegs, perishers, roughs, hard
boys, street ruffians, young tearaways** —
hoodlums
twister, flicker, waster, footpad — crook

Holidays
The legal holidays are called **Bank Holidays** because
on these days, the banks are closed by Act of
Parliament. They are held on Mondays in the better
weather part of the year to make for long weekends.
For most of Britain, the Bank Holidays are:
January 1 — New Year's Day

Good Friday Bank Holiday

Easter is a moveable holiday as it is celebrated on the first Sunday after the full moon, between March 22 and April 25.

Easter Monday Bank Holiday (except Scotland)

May (First Mon) — May Day Bank Holiday

May (Last Mon) — Spring Bank Holiday

August (Last Mon) — Summer Bank Holiday (except Scotland)

December 25 — Christmas Day Bank Holiday

Boxing Day Bank Holiday — day after Christmas except if it occurs on Saturday or Sunday, then it's on the following Monday

SCOTLAND ONLY:

January 3 — Bank Holiday

January 25 — Burns Night

August (First Mon) — Summer Bank Holiday

October 30 — Halloween

November 5 — Bonfire Night

November 28 — St Andrew's Day

December 31 — Hogmanay

IRELAND ONLY:

December 28 — Feast of the Holy Innocents or Children's Day

March 17 — St. Patrick's Day

May 1 — May Day

June 24 — Feast of St. John

July (2nd Mon) — Orangeman's Day (Northern Ireland only)

September 29 — Michaelmas

CYMRU (WALES) ONLY:

March 1 — St. David's Day

In July — the Royal National Eisteddfodau of Wales, a festival of music and song

The Law

The Inns of Court are four societies (**The Inner Temple,** the **Middle Temple, Lincoln's Inn** and **Gray's Inn**) that have the exclusive right of **calling to the bar** (giving bar examination) to those who wish to become **barristers** or **solicitors.** Here's another instance where the English language diverges. Our solicitors are salesmen, their solicitors are lawyers who can plead in a Lower Court. Barristers can plead before both Lower and Higher Courts and can **"take silk,"** that is, in time, they can get to wear a silk robe and wig in court and have **Q.C.** (Queen's Counsel) appended to their names. The Inns are law universities and have kept the name **"Inns"** (tradition again) from the time they once furnished permanent residence for their members.

THE LONG ROBE (LEGAL PROFESSION) TERMS

adjudicators — judges
attorney-in-fact, private attorney — attorney
in Chancery — in litigation
Clerk of the Peace (C.P.) — Justice of the Peace
cross question — cross examine
Deed Poll — Court Order
Duty Solicitor — Public Defender
hard swearing — perjury
High Bailiff — server of **writs** (summons)
Legacy Duties — Death Duties
lodge an appeal — file an appeal
not in the dock — not on trial
Objection allowed! — Objection sustained!
on one's own showing — on one's own statement
Queen's/King's Bench — a division of the High
   Court of Justice
situation, a — a case
succession duty — inheritance tax

swear an information — make a formal complaint
ticket-of-leave — suspended sentence
turn Queen's/King's evidence — turn state's
  evidence
undertaking — agreement
Westminster Hall — Court of Justice
witness box — witness stand
You may stand down. — You may step down.

The Royals

At the outbreak of WWI, King George V, Queen Elizabeth's grandfather, cut off all ties with Germany by the symbolic act of removing himself from the Hanoverian line of British regents. Taking the name from Windsor Castle, he called his line **The House of Windsor.** His son, Edward VIII succeeded him and when he abdicated to marry Mrs. Wallis Warfield Simpson, Elizabeth's father became George VI. Elizabeth became Queen in 1952. She and her husband, Prince Philip of Greece are both great, great grandchildren of Queen Victoria. Their children are Charles, Prince of Wales, Princess Anne, Prince Andrew and Prince Edward.

The UK is a parliamentary democracy, that is, the Prime Minister and his Cabinet wield executive powers; however, legislation can only become law by the assent of the Queen who is Head of State. She has the power of veto but no regent has ever exercised a veto in over 280 years. The Queen, who has a sharp, retentive mind, receives a Red Box every day which contains all the doings of the Cabinet, and she confers with the Prime Minister every Tuesday night.

Prime Ministers and Cabinets come and go but the Queen stays on representing stability when Parliament is out of session. She is well loved, not only for herself but because she represents tradition...and tradition is the UK's middle name.

WORDS DEALING WITH ROYALTY

Black Rod — an usher of the House of Lords who carries an ebony stick with which to knock three times on the door of the Commons to summon them to the state opening of Parliament.

Blues and Royals and **Life Guards** — cavalry brigades of the British Household who ride beside and before the Royal Carriage on state occasions

Buck House — Buckingham Palace

Cap of Maintenance — a cap worn by or carried before a person of rank proclaiming his/her high office

Gentlemen of the Privy Chamber — officials in the royal household in attendance at court

Goldstick — a colonel of the Life Guards who carries a gilded wand before the Sovereign

H.M. — Her Majesty

King-at-Arms — herald who reads royal proclamations

Life Peer — one whose title is not hereditary

Lords and Ladies of the Bedchamber — officers of the royal household who wait, in turn, upon the sovereign

Privy Purse — allowance for a sovereign's private expenses

Right Honourable — title given to the following: peers below the rank of Marquis, privy-councillors, present and past cabinet ministers and to certain Lord Mayors and Lord provosts

Silver Stick — a palace officer who carries a silver wand

St. Edward's Crown — symbol of monarchy which has been used for crowning all the kings and queens since Charles II, except for Queen Victoria, for whom the Imperial State Crown was made

Stone of Scone, Stone of Destiny, or Coronation Stone — the stone on which ancient Celtic kings had been crowned which was taken from Scotland by Edward I in 1296 when he conquered Scotland

and proclamed himself King of Scotland. The 450-pound block of sandstone rests under the seat of the Coronation Chair in Westminster Abbey.

The Hons. — short for Honorables, the sons and daughters of peers

The Household — the royal domestic establishment

Worthiest of Blood — a term used in a question of succession, meaning, male supercedes female

ENTERTAINMENT

Theater

London is called the theater capital of the world. There are 37 alone in the West End, others are on the South Bank near Waterloo and still others in the heart of the City. Half price tickets can be bought from a **booking clerk** (ticket agent) at the **Leicester Square Half-Price Ticket Booth** which levies a service charge of up to £1.50 for any seats unsold **on the day of the performance.** There are no phone numbers for this Ticket Booth; one must appear in person at 12 noon for matinee tickets and 14:30 to 18:30 (2:30 to 6:30) for evening performances. Special pre-theater dinners can be had at many West End restaurants.

THEATER WORDS

boards, the — the stage

bomb — a hit

candy butchers — candy sellers

comic turn, comedy chat — comedy routine

cruncher, the — the punchline

crush bars — buffets (in larger theaters)

dress circle — mezzanine

gangway — aisles

gallery — second balcony

Intervals — Intermissions

orchestra stalls — the first two or three rows

stalls — the regular seats

stalls bars — refreshment stands
star turn — the star
straight play — a play without music
top-liner — headliner
try it on the dog audience — preview audience
turn, a — a performer
upper circle — the first balcony

FOOD AND DRINK

The British have had a bad rap regarding haute cuisine. They've been praised for their hearty breakfasts, traditional roast beef and Yorkshire pudding dinners, their pub lunches and especially their teas with mouth watering assortments of sandwiches and cakes. What has often been overlooked is that there are many wonderful regional dishes to enjoy such as: Scotland's delicious cock-a-leekie soup, Wales' honeyed Welsh lamb, the West Country's yummy Cornish pasty, the South's famous Dover sole, the Midland's shepherd pie, the North-west's hot pot and Ireland's excellent Irish stew. Also, Britain has had an influx of restaurants featuring foreign cuisine, plus a good number of the US' fast food establishments.

The British, like most Europeans, use the knife and fork in a very efficient way. The fork is held by the left hand with the tines held down, and when a piece of food is cut, it is transferred to the mouth directly by the same left hand, so it is in place for the next forkful. Mashed potatoes are used as a "mortar" by the knife to hold slippery foods, such as peas, in place.

Pubs

Most visitors to the U.K. want the experience of visiting a **public house**, affectionately known as the **"pub"** or **"the local."** There are more than 70,000 in the UK and they are patronized by both sexes. Most pubs are very warm and inviting with fireplaces, wooden tables, beveled glass, and decorations that have stood the test of time. They are traditional social meeting places. Some have family rooms where children of all ages can accompany their parents. Children aged 14 to 17 can be admitted alone to pubs to get non-alcoholic drinks but one must be 18 to be served alcohol. **"The Snug"** is a small room reserved for regulars and trespassing is strictly taboo.

A pub lunch is an economical alternative to an American fast-food establishment. Try the **Plowman's Lunch** (a chunk of delicious country bread served with either a large chunk of cheese, pickles, butter and tea or slices of roast beef, tomato and lettuce.) Another good choice is **Shepherd's Pie** made with ground beef topped with mashed potatoes. Don't fail to try the delicious pickled eggs. Mmm!

PUB HOURS

England and Wales:
Weekdays: 11:00 - 23:00 (11:00)
Sundays: 12:00 - 15:00 (3:00)
19:00 (7:00) p.m. to 22:30 (10:30)
Scotland:
Weekdays: 11:00 - 23:00 (11:00)
Sundays: 12:30 -14:30 (2:30)
18:30 (6:30) - 23:00 (11:00)
Northern Ireland:
Weekdays: 11:30 - 23:00 (11:00)
Sundays: 12:30 - 14:00 (2:00)
19:00 (7:00) - 22:00 (10:00)

Note: Some country pubs may close afternoons from 15:00 (3:00) - 17:30 (5:30); others are now open all day, following the practice of Continental establishments in the Common Market; that is, from 10:30/11:00 for 12 hours, without the afternoon break. To do so is the choice of the landlord or the barman's employer.

PUB OFFERINGS

athole brose — a whisky and honey mixture

banana split — half bitter and half lager

barley wine — beer with a high alcohol content

bitter beer — pale ale

bitter top — pint of bitter topped with an inch of 7-UP

black and tan — stout and bitter beer

black beer — black syrupy Danzig beer

black eye — rum and brandy

black velvet — stout and champagne or half bitter/ half cider

Bristol milk — sherry

brown beer — weak beer

bumbo — mix of rum or gin with water, sugar and nutmeg

cape smoke — South African brandy

cider — hard cider or applejack

cider-cup — cider with spices, sugar and ice

cider and — cider and spirits

claret-cup — iced claret, brandy and sugar

cobbler's punch — warm beer with spirits, sugar and spice

cold without — brandy with cold water

dog's nose — gin and beer

egg-flip — ale, wine, spirits or milk with eggs, sugar and spices

G & T — gin and tonic

ginger beer — effervescent ginger drink

ginger-cordial — cordial of ginger, lemon peel, raisins, water and sometimes liquor

half and half — half porter/ half ale

hot toddy — a shot of scotch with sugar, lemon juice and hot water

jorum — a stiff drink

log juice — bad port wine

mild beer — the weakest draft beer

Mother's ruin, blue ruin, What killed Auntie?, or **old Tom** — gin

peg — brandy and soda

pint of mild and bitter — half mild, half bitter on tap

porter — bock beer

red biddy — red wine and whisky

rum and black — rum and black currant juice

scrumpy or **rough cider** — very alcoholic, flat, non-fizzy cider

shandy — half beer/ half lemonade

snakebite — half bitter and half alcoholic cider

snowball — a mix of advocat (egg yolks and brandy), lime juice and 7 UP

squash — fruit syrup and water

stout ale — beer made from hops and brown sugar

twist — mixed drink

whiskey — Irish whisky

whiskey-mack — whisky and ginger beer

whiskey and splash — whisky and soda or seltzer

whiskey toddy — toddy with whisky as the chief ingredient

white ale — whitish ale brewed or mixed with flour or eggs

Restaurants

APPROXIMATE U.K. MEAL TIMES

Breakfast — 7:30 to 9 a.m.
Lunch — 12 to 2
Tea — 4 to 5
High Tea — 6 p.m. (takes the place of dinner)
Dinner — 7:30 to 9:30 p.m.

Important: Look for The Restaurant Customers' Charter, a sign in a restaurant window which guarantees a fixed price menu and indicates whether or not a service charge is included. Bread and butter are not usually served with a meal. They are considered extras. Water, also, must be asked for when giving an order.

RESTAURANT WORDS

afters — desserts

chips — French fries

feeling peckish, sharpset or **ravening** — feeling hungry

hot and hot — term for foods cooked and served in hot dishes

plonk — house wine

pusher — piece of bread used for pushing food onto a fork

sugar caster — sugar shaker

starters — appetizers

the bill — the check

The Gents' Cloaks or **Ladies' Cloaks** — restrooms

to book a table — to make a reservation

RESTAURANT FOODS

ENTREES

angels on horseback — skewered oysters wrapped in bacon

archangels on horseback — scallops wrapped in bacon and broiled

bangers and mash — sausage and mashed potatoes

beef alamode — beef larded and stewed with vegetables

Bidlington rarebit — very rich cheese sauce on soft buttered toast flavored with nutmeg

bubble and squeak — slices of warmed cold beef covered with a fried mixture of cabbage and onion

canape' Diane — chicken livers wrapped in bacon and served on toast

cider glazed gammon — mildly cured ham cooked with hard cider and served with spiced peaches

devil's on horseback — kidneys wrapped in bacon

Exeter stew — chopped beef, onions, carrots and herbs

faggots — spiced meat balls containing pig's liver

guard of honour — roast lamb with the bones crossing each other like swords

jemmy — baked sheep's head

Kentish bacon roly poly — chopped bacon, onion and spices spread out on dough and rolled jelly-roll fashion, wrapped in foil and steamed; then served with a vegetable mix

Lancashire hot pot — lamb and kidney pot pie covered with sliced potatoes and baked

potted chicken — creamed chicken mixed with lemon juice, parsley, salt and pepper and served in ramekins

potted shrimp — tiny Morecambe Bay shrimp coated with clarified butter

sausage and mash — sausage and mashed potatoes

scotch woodcock — scrambled eggs flavored with anchovy paste and served on toast

steak and kidney pudding — steak and kidney stew covered with pastry

toad-in-the-hole — Yorkshire pudding topped with sausages

VEGETABLES

jacket potato — baked potato

swedes — rutabagas

windsor beans — broad beans

BREADS

Barm Brack — round loaf made with self-rising flour, tea, brown sugar and dried fruit

brown bread — wholewheat or rye bread

cobloaf — round loaf of bread

Country Baps — rolls resembling hamburger rolls

French sticks — French bread

Indian bread — chappati or noam

maize bread — corn bread

malt loaf — yeast bread made with malt extract and **black treacle** (a sort of molasses)

torpedoes — frankfurter-like buns used as biscuits

DESSERTS

These usually arrive at the table on a dessert trolley (dessert wagon). Custards and whipped cream are usually available to embellish cake.

Apple Snow — apple puree mixed with beaten egg white and served with custard

Bakewell Tart — raspberry jam spread on a pastry base with an almond mixture over all; occasionally topped with a **pastry-grid** (lattice-top)

Battenberg Cake — vanilla-flavored and raspberry-flavored sponge cakes cut into cubes and joined together with jam in a four-square design

Bilberry Pie — blueberry pie

Bramble Pudding — blackberry compote with apple slices

Brown Pudding — boiled pudding with dried fruit, ground almonds and spices

Butter Sponge — sponge cake made with butter; some are plain, others are made with lemon, strawberries or chocolate

Canary Pudding — lemon pudding

Castle Puddings — individual **sponges** (sponge cakes) served with jam sauce

Crumble — fruit cobbler like apple crisp

Cabinet Pudding — custard, candied fruit preserves and ladyfingers

Eve's Pudding — baked apple slices topped with sponge cake batter

Flummery — almond-flavored jelly that's delicious with strawberries

Gooseberry Pie

Roly-Poly Pudding — rolled suet cake, steamed

Rum Nicky — a sticky tart made of dates and ginger

Summer Pudding — bread mixed with fruit

Sponge Sandwich — jelly roll

Syllabub — mixture of lemon, sweet sherry, brandy and sugar topped with whipped cream

Treacle Tart — like pecan pie without the pecans

Trifle — sponge cake slices sandwiched together with raspberry or strawberry jam, doused with sherry and then covered with custard to an inch or two in depth and then topped with whipped cream. Teetotallers use orange or other fruit juice for sherry...but it's not the same.

ALTERNATIVE DESSERT CHOICES

Cheese: Britain is noted for its delicious cheeses. Americans are familiar with Stilton blue but there's also a delicious creamy Stilton white which is too delicate to export. Other cheeses to try are: Leicester Red (yellow color), Wensleydale, Derbyshire, Double Gloucester, and Cheddar.

Savoury: a small portion of a seasoned dish like Welsh Rabbit

Fast Foods:

beans on toast — baked beans on toast

bread and dripping — fat poured off a roast, allowed to cool and set before being spread on bread

breadberry — bread and hot milk

bangers and bittersloater — sausages and beer

cornet — ice cream cone

fish and chips — sold at a **Chippy** (Fish and Chips Shop)

fish fingers — fish sticks

fish cake — fish croquette

hot sausage sandwich

Melton Mowbray pie or **Pork Pie** — well seasoned chopped pork in a pie shell, eaten cold

Priddy-oggies — pastry turnovers filled with pork and cheddar

sausage rolls — sausages in pastry. They are made two ways: **"Puff"** and **"Short."** Puff pastry is oilier, having a greater fat content; short pastry is more biscuit-like.

slide — ice cream sandwich

Tea

"Everything stops for tea" is a popular British saying. Tea time can be any time of the day but as a rule, many have tea instead of coffee for breakfast and afternoon tea between 4 and 5. Scottish high tea is at 5 p.m.

Tea choices: Simple Teas and **Cream Teas** consist of hot scones with butter, jam and delicious Devonshire Cream. **High Teas** have a mixture of foods: wafer thin cucumber or watercress sandwiches, sardine and tomato sandwiches, creamed foods on toast, small pieces of cold meat or fish, egg dishes, salads, scones, small cakes, tarts, shortbreads, whipped cream, jam and pudding. **"Meat teas"** are high teas with meats.

TEA OFFERINGS

Abernethy biscuits — caraway seed cookies

Alma tea cakes — cookies made on a griddle

Bakewell tarts — almond cakes with a filling of raspberry preserves

Banbury cakes — oval currant and spice tarts

bannock — flat, round, unleavened oat biscuits made on a griddle

Bath-buns — raisin buns

Bath Oliver — biscuits invented by Dr. W. Oliver of Bath, excellent with cheese

Chelsea buns — sticky buns with dried fruit and honey glaze

Dundee cake — cake made with almonds, cherries, dried fruit and lemon peel

Eccles cakes — similar to Banbury cakes

fairy cakes or **queen cakes**— cupcakes topped with icing and a cherry

ginger nuts — ginger cookies

jam doughnut — jelly doughnut

Yorkshire parkin — oatmeal, ginger and treacle cake

rock cakes — dried fruit buns with shortening worked in as when making shortbread

SHOPPING

Many Americans go to the U.K. just to shop, expecially for its superb woolens that last a lifetime and its world-renowned china and pottery. Antiques are also a great attraction. Shopping centers are called **"Shopping Parades."** A **"parade"** in the UK is not only the kind one is familiar with but it can also be a **"promenade"** or a **"display."** In this case, it is a display of **"shops,"** their name for "stores." **"Stores"** are storage places or warehouses. Most shops are open from 9:00 to 5:30, Mondays to Saturdays; and some department stores may stay open one day a week until 8:00 at night.

Note: Small towns may have a 1 p.m. closing one day a week and may also close for lunch the other days.

SHOPPING WORDS

cash and wrap — cash and carry
carriage free service — free delivery
cost price, trade price — at cost, wholesale
fire clearance sale — fire sale
on tick, on the slate — on credit
pricey, posh — dear, expensive
purchase tax — sales tax
Reduced to Clear — Clearance Sale
shop walker — floor walker
the latest shout — the latest fashion
the never-never — the installment plan
the try-on — the fitting
to attend to — to wait on

SIZES

Women's Dresses, Blouses, Knitwear, Lingerie									
U.K	8	10	12	14	16	18	20	22	24
U.S	6	8	10	12	14	16	18	20	22
To fit bust (inches)	34	36	38	40	42	44	46	48	50

Men's Suits, Overcoats , Sweaters, Shirts and Collars
The same as in the U.S.

Women's Shoe Sizes:

U.K.	3	4	4½	5	5½	6	6½	7	7½	8
U.S.		4½	5½	6	6½	7	7½	8	8½	9	9½

Men's Shoe Sizes:

U.K	5	6	7	8	9	10	11
U.S.	5½	6½	7 ½	8½	9½	10 ½	11½

WEARING APPAREL WORDS

SHOES

court shoes — pumps
dress wellingtons — long legged elegant boots for military evening dress
high-lows — high shoes fastened in front
jackboots — boots reaching above the knee
kidskin — calfskin
mutton dummies — white sneakers
plimsolls — sneakers
slop in — scuffs
undress shoes, carpet slippers — bedroom slippers

winkle pickers — shoes with pointed toes

CHILDREN'S WEAR
Alice band — hair band
balaclava — woolen hat covering the ears and back of the head
gaufer-stitched smock — ruffled or fluted smock
kissing strings — cap or bonnet strings

WOMEN'S WEAR
briefs or **knickers** — panties
Cami-knickers — teddys, body briefers
frock — dress
jumper — pullover sweater
minikinis — bikini panties
overall — smock
pinny, pinafore — jumper
smock frock — smock
towelling wrap — terry robe
waist slip — half slip
woolies — jumpers, jerseys, warm undervests
wrap-around — overall apron
wrapover frock — wraparound dress

WOMEN'S ACCESSORIES
crocodile-skin handbag — alligator bag
Dorothy bag — drawstring bag, tote
head hugger, head scarf, head square — kerchief
ladies' purse notecase — wallet

MEN'S WEAR
cheese cutter — square peaked hat
camelcloth coat — camel's hair coat
drape suit — long jacket and narrow pants
dressing gown — robe
gilets, waistcoats — vests
great coat — overcoat
guernsey, gansey — fisherman's sweater made of waterproof oiled wool in traditional Island of Guernsey designs.

IMPORTANT ADDRESSES AND TELEPHONE NUMBERS

EMERGENCIES:

U.S.

U.K.

Citizen's Emergency Center
Washington, D.C.
1-202-647-5225

American Embassy,
London
24-31 Grosvenor Square
44-0171-499-9000
Fax: 44-0171-495-5012

TRAVEL INFORMATION:

U.S.

U.K.

British Consulate
845 Third Avenue
New York, N.Y. 10022
1-212-745-0200

British Travel Authority (BTA)
551 Fifth Avenue, Suite 701
New York, N.Y. 10176
1-212-986-2200
There are BTA offices in Atlanta,
Georgia, Chicago and Los Angeles
At same address:
Northern Ireland Tourist Board
1-212-922-0101 or 1-800-326-0036

Republic of Ireland information:
Irish Tourist Board
345 Park Ave, 17th Floor (51st St),
New York, N.Y. 10154
1-212-418-0800 or 1-800-223-6470

BritRail Travel Intl. Inc.
1500 Broadway
New York, N.Y. 10036
1-212-575-2667

British Travel Bookshop
Box 1224
Clifton, N.J. 07012
1-800-448-3039
1-212-490-6688

British Travel Centre
12 Regent Street
Picadilly Circus
London SW1Y 4PQ
(Appear in person)
At same address:
Wales Tourist Board
(0171) 409-0969

Scottish Tourist Board
17 Cockspur Street
London SW1
(0171) 930-8661

Northern Ireland Tourist
Board
11 Berkeley Steet
London W1
(0171) 493-0601

winkle pickers — shoes with pointed toes

CHILDREN'S WEAR
Alice band — hair band
balaclava — woolen hat covering the ears and back of the head
gaufer-stitched smock — ruffled or fluted smock
kissing strings — cap or bonnet strings

WOMEN'S WEAR
briefs or **knickers** — panties
Cami-knickers — teddys, body briefers
frock — dress
jumper — pullover sweater
minikinis — bikini panties
overall — smock
pinny, pinafore — jumper
smock frock — smock
towelling wrap — terry robe
waist slip — half slip
woolies — jumpers, jerseys, warm undervests
wrap-around — overall apron
wrapover frock — wraparound dress

WOMEN'S ACCESSORIES
crocodile-skin handbag — alligator bag
Dorothy bag — drawstring bag, tote
head hugger, head scarf, head square — kerchief
ladies' purse notecase — wallet

MEN'S WEAR
cheese cutter — square peaked hat
camelcloth coat — camel's hair coat
drape suit — long jacket and narrow pants
dressing gown — robe
gilets, waistcoats — vests
great coat — overcoat
guernsey, gansey — fisherman's sweater made of waterproof oiled wool in traditional Island of Guernsey designs.

jemmy — coat

Newmarket — close-fitting coat, originally a riding coat; named after Newmarket, a racing town

jumper — pullover

plus-fours — baggy knickerbocker suit

polo neck sweater — turtleneck sweater

singlet — undershirt

slipover — sleeveless sweater

smalls, pants, small clothes, underneaths — shorts

trews — trousers in a Clan Tartan

vests — undershirts

MEN'S ACCESSORIES

billycock — bowler-type hat

bootlace tie — string tie

braces — suspenders

buttonhole — boutonniere

chimney pot hat, plug hat, topper, silk hat — top hat

chip hat — hat of palm strips

note case, notebook, pocket bookman's — wallet, billfold

quizzing glass — monocle on a stick

trilby, trilby hat — fedora

wideawake hat — low, wide-brimmed canvas or soft felt hat

JEWELRY

Bristol diamonds — quartz crystals found near Bristol

earbobs — earrings

mascot — charm for charm bracelet

starstone — star sapphire

RAINWEAR

brolly — umbrella, bumbershoot

derriboots, half-wellingtons — short rubber boots

india rubber boots, gum boots — rubber boots

mack, mackintosh, waterproof — raincoat

IMPORTANT ADDRESSES AND TELEPHONE NUMBERS

EMERGENCIES:

U.S.

Citizen's Emergency Center
Washington, D.C.
1-202-647-5225

U.K.

American Embassy,
London
24-31 Grosvenor Square
44-0171-499-9000
Fax: 44-0171-495-5012

TRAVEL INFORMATION:

U.S.

British Consulate
845 Third Avenue
New York, N.Y. 10022
1-212-745-0200

British Travel Authority (BTA)
551 Fifth Avenue, Suite 701
New York, N.Y. 10176
1-212-986-2200
There are BTA offices in Atlanta,
Georgia, Chicago and Los Angeles
At same address:
Northern Ireland Tourist Board
1-212-922-0101 or 1-800-326-0036

Republic of Ireland information:
Irish Tourist Board
345 Park Ave, 17th Floor (51st St),
New York, N.Y. 10154
1-212-418-0800 or 1-800-223-6470

BritRail Travel Intl. Inc.
1500 Broadway
New York, N.Y. 10036
1-212-575-2667

British Travel Bookshop
Box 1224
Clifton, N.J. 07012
1-800-448-3039
1-212-490-6688

U.K.

British Travel Centre
12 Regent Street
Picadilly Circus
London SW1Y 4PQ
(Appear in person)
At same address:
Wales Tourist Board
(0171) 409-0969

Scottish Tourist Board
17 Cockspur Street
London SW1
(0171) 930-8661

**Northern Ireland Tourist
Board**
11 Berkeley Steet
London W1
(0171) 493-0601

ulsters and toppers — overcoats and hats of rain proof tweed

wellingtons — generic name for rubber boots

SPORTS WEAR

anorak — parka

games tunic — gym suit

hacking jacket — riding jacket

P.E. shorts, P.T. shorts — athletic shorts

polo neck pullover, roll-neck pullover — turtleneck sweater

shooting coat — hunting jacket

snow spectacles — snow goggles

tanga — string bikini

thrum cap — cap made of coarse, shaggy cloth

trainers — gym shoes or sneakers

windcheater — windbreaker

International Literature with Hippocrene Books

**DEDALUS BOOK OF
MEDIEVAL LITERATURE:
THE GRIN OF THE GARGOYLE**
edited by Brian Murdoch
265 pgs, 5 1/2 x 8 1/2, 1-873982-02-X
$16.95pb (299)

**DEDALUS BOOK OF SURREALISM I:
THE IDENTITY OF THINGS**
edited by Michael Richardson
384 pgs, 5 1/2 x 8 1/2, 1-873982-45-3
$16.95pb (179)

**DEDALUS BOOK OF SURREALISM II:
THE MYTH OF THE WORLLD**
edited by Michael Richardson
320 pgs, 5 1/2 x 8 1/2, 1-873982-36-4
$16.95pb (22)

ACTS OF THE APOSTATES
written by Geoffrey Farrington
272 pgs, 5 x 8, 0-94662-646-4
$11.95pb (409)

THE ARABIAN NIGHTMARE
written by Robert Irwin
302 pgs, 4 1/2 x 7, 1-873982-05-4
$12.95pb (588)

**THE DEDALUS BOOK OF
BRITISH FANTASY:
THE NINETEENTH CENTURY**
edited by Brian Stableford
416 pgs, 5 1/2 x 8 1/2, 1-946626-78-2
$14.95pb (403)

**THE DEDALUS BOOK OF
DECADENCE:
MORAL RUINS**
Revised edition
edited by Brian Stableford
288 pgs, 5 1/2 x 8 1/2, 1-873982-01-1
$14.95pb (101)

**THE DEDALUS BOOK OF
FEMMES FATALES**
edited by Brian Stableford
288 pgs, 5 1/2 x 8 1/2, 0-946626-72-4
$14.95pb (81)

THE EPISODES OF VATHEK
written by William Beckford
208 pgs, 5 1/2 x 8 1/2, 1-873982-61-5
$16.95pb (454)

THE SECOND DEDALUS
BOOK OF DECADENCE:
THE BLACK FEAST
edited by Brian Stableford
356 pgs, 5 1/2 x 8 1/2, 0-946626-80-4
$14.95pb (105)

TRAVELS WITH MYSELF AND
ANOTHER
written by Martha Gelhorn
284 pgs, 5 1/2 x 8 1/2, 0-90787-135-0
$14.95pb (433)

HIPPOCRENE HANDY DICTIONARIES

For the traveler of independent spirit and curious mind,
this practical series will help you to communicate, not
just to get by.

All titles: 120 pages, 5" x 7", $8.95 paper

ARABIC
0463 • 0-87052-960-9

PORTUGUESE
0324 • 0-87052-053-9

CHINESE
0347 • 0-87052-050-4

RUSSIAN
0371 • 0-7818-0013-7

DUTCH
0323 • 0-87052-049-0

SERBO-CROATIAN
0328 • 0-87052-051-2

FRENCH
0155 • 0-7818-0010-2

SLOVAK
0359 • 0-7818-0101-X
* *$12.95*

GERMAN
0378 • 0-7818-0014-5

SPANISH
0189 • 0-7818-0012-9

GREEK
0464 • 0-87052-961-7

SWEDISH
0345 • 0-87052-054-7

ITALIAN
0196 • 0-7818-0011-0

THAI
0468 • 0-87052-963-3

JAPANESE
0466 • 0-87052-962-5

TURKISH
0375 • 0-87052-982-X

KOREAN
0438 • 0-7818-0082-X

All prices subject to change.)
**TO PURCHASE HIPPOCRENE BOOKS contact your local
bookstore, or write to: HIPPOCRENE BOOKS, 171 Madison
Avenue, New York, NY 10016. Please enclose check or money
order, adding $5.00 shipping (UPS) for the first book and $.50 for
each additional book.**

HIPPOCRENE MASTERING SERIES

This teach-yourself language series, now available in 9 languages, is perfect for the serious traveler, student or businessperson.

MASTERING ARABIC
0-87052-922-6
$14.95pb
2 Cassettes
0-87052-984-6 $12.95

MASTERING JAPANESE
0-87052-923-4
$14.95pb
2 Cassettes
0-87052-938-8 $12.95

MASTERING FINNISH
0-7818-0233-4
$14.95pb
2 Cassettes
0-7818-0265-2 $12.95

MASTERING POLISH
0-7818-0015-3
$14.95pb
2 Cassettes
0-7818-0016-3 $12.95

MASTERING FRENCH
0-87052-055-5
$11.95pb
2 Cassettes
0-87052-060-1 $12.95

MASTERING RUSSIAN
0-7818-0270-9
$14.95pb
2 Cassettes
0-7818-0270-9 $12.95

MASTERING GERMAN
0-87052-056-3
$11.95pb
2 Cassettes
0-87052-061-X $12.95

MASTERING SPANISH
0-87052-059-8
$11.95pb
2 Cassettes
0-87052-067-9 $12.95

MASTERING ITALIAN
0-87052-057-1
$11.95pb
2 Cassettes
0-87052-066-0 $12.95

All prices subject to change. **TO PURCHASE HIPPOCRENE BOOKS**, contact your local bookstore, or write to: HIPPOCRENE BOOKS, 171 Madison Avenue, New York, NY 10016. Please enclose check or money order, adding $5.00 shipping (UPS) for the first book and $.50 for each additional book.